ENJOYING
POETRY

ENJOYING
POETRY

SADLER, HAYLLAR, POWELL

M

First published 1981 by
THE MACMILLAN COMPANY OF AUSTRALIA PTY LTD
107 Moray Street, South Melbourne 3205
6 Clarke Street, Crows Nest 2065
Reprinted 1981 (twice)

Associated companies in
London and Basingstoke, England
Auckland Dallas Delhi Hong Kong
Johannesburg Lagos Manzini Nairobi
New York Singapore Tokyo Washington Zaria

National Library of Australia
cataloguing in publication data
Sadler, R. K. (Rex Kevin)
    Enjoying poetry.
    Index
    ISBN 0 333 29972 8
    1. English poetry. I. Hayllar, T. A. S.
    (Thomas Albert S.). II. Powell, C. J.
    (Clifford J.). III. Title.
821'.008

Set in Century by Savage & Co. Pty Ltd, Brisbane

Printed in Hong Kong
by South China Printing Co.

Illustrated by Julia Wakefield

Additional art by Julie Gross
Cover: Jim Lim

Contents

Contents

9. City Life 85

10. Writing Your First Poems 95

11. A Humorous Look at Ourselves 101

12. Rhythm 121

13. Strange Happenings 129

14. Alliteration 143

Contents

19. Birds of Feather   179

20. Ogden Nash   187

21. War   191

22. Unhappy Little Poems   199

Contents

Preface

A poem is not a delicate piece of pottery that
clumsy hands may drop and break in pieces. It
can be analysed, dissected, put under the
microscope; and the closer and more detailed
the examination, the more one finds to admire,
as with any work of art.

from *Feet on the Ground*
by Margaret J. O'Donnell

Poetry, like other fine arts, exists to be enjoyed and appreciated. The difficult task facing any teacher is that of developing this sense of appreciation and enjoyment in students who initially 'don't like poetry'.

Obviously, to some extent appreciation grows out of understanding. Students must learn to examine poems critically and thoughtfully, to see what the poet is driving at, to consider how well he or she is saying it, and so on. This does require work of some sort, but there is no other way to develop appreciation of poetry. The work can be at the talking level, with teachers and students discussing aspects of a poem and trying to refine their awareness of its impact on them by thoughtful analysis. It can also be at the writing level, with students attentively evaluating and communicating, in written form, the achievement and effect of a poem.

A sensitive teaching approach is needed — one that combines discussion and writing, one that examines ideas and feelings, one that encourages appreciation of the poetry of others while also giving room for the student to try his or her own hand at creating poetry — an approach that above all is built upon teacher-enthusiasm for poetry.

In this book, we have tried to offer raw material which we believe can be shaped into a poetry course aimed at developing an appreciation and an enjoyment of poetry. In particular, we have tried to present material that carries a high level of interest for students, while not neglecting the needs of quality. Furthermore, special units — on topics such as simile and metaphor, personification, alliteration, rhyme, rhythm, poetry-writing — appear throughout the book and provide a way of introducing students to the basics of poetry technique. In short, we believe that teachers will find this to be a poetry book that students can learn from and enjoy.

With poetry, as with many other pursuits in life, understanding brings enjoyment.

1. Our Land

One of the most recited poems in Australian literature is Dorothea Mackellar's 'My Country'. It is not as popular today as in the past. Can you suggest why?

MY COUNTRY

The love of field and coppice,
  Of green and shaded lanes,
Of ordered woods and gardens
  Is running in your veins;
Strong love of grey-blue distance,
  Brown streams and soft, dim skies —
I know but cannot share it,
  My love is otherwise.

I love a sunburnt country,
  A land of sweeping plains,
Of ragged mountain ranges,
  Of droughts and flooding rains;
I love her far horizons,
  I love her jewel-sea,
Her beauty and her terror —
  The wide brown land for me.

The tragic ring-barked forests
  Stark white beneath the moon,
The sapphire-misted mountains,
  The hot gold hush of noon.
Green tangle of the brushes
  Where lithe lianas coil,
And orchids deck the tree-tops
  And ferns the crimson soil.

Core of my heart, my country!
  Her pitiless blue sky,
When sick at heart around us
  We see the cattle die —
But then the grey clouds gather
  And we can bless again
The drumming of an army,
  The steady, soaking rain.

Core of my heart, my country!
  Land of the Rainbow Gold,
Of flood and fire and famine,
  She pays us back threefold;
Over the thirsty paddocks,
  Watch, after many days,
The filmy veil of greenness
  That thickens as we gaze.

An opal-hearted country,
  A wilful, lavish land —
All you who have not loved her,
  You will not understand —
Though earth holds many splendours,
  Wherever I may die,
I know to what brown country
  My homing thoughts will fly.

DOROTHEA MACKELLAR

Poet's Corner

One day when I was nineteen I was talking with a friend of the same age about the anti-Australianism — commoner then than now — of many Australians we knew. We both vehemently disliked it, and I went straight home from her house with verses ringing in my head.

Several friends saw the result, and persuaded me to send it to *The Spectator* (London), where it was published.

Dorothea Mackellar

My Country — A comparison

Oscar Krahnvohl's version of 'My Country' appeared more than seventy years after Dorothea Mackellar's poem had been published. Whose view of Australia do you think is the truer — Mackellar's or Krahnvohl's? Why? Which of the two poems appeals to you more? Can you suggest in what ways Oscar Krahnvohl has taken some of his ideas from the original 'My Country'?

MY COUNTRY

I love a sunburnt country,
A land of open drains
Mid-urban sprawl expanded
For cost-accounting gains;
Broad, busy bulldozed acres
Once wastes of fern and trees
Now rapidly enriching
Investors overseas.

A nature-loving country
Beneath whose golden wattles
The creek is fringed with newspapers
And lined with broken bottles.
Far in her distant outback
Still whose cities chafe
Find hidden pools where bathing
Is relatively safe.

A music-loving country
Where rings throughout the land
The jingle sweet enjoining
Devotion to the brand.
O, hark the glad transistors
Whence midnight, dawn and noon
Cry forth her U.S. idols
A trifle out of tune.

Brave military pylons
That march o'er scenic hills;
Fair neon lights, extolling
Paint, puppy food and pills!
I love her massive chimneys,
Production's, profit's pride,
Interminably pouring
Pollution high and wide.

A democratic country
Where, safe from fear's attacks,
Earth's children all are equal
(Save yellows, browns and blacks).
Though Man in Space adventure,
Invade the planets nine,
What shall he find to equal
This sunburnt land of mine?

OSCAR KRAHNVOHL

A confident team — consisting of Harry, his saddle-horse, his packhorse and his dog — moves home across the plains, unaware that they are about to confront one of the deadliest dangers of the outback.

THE BALLAD OF THE DROVER

Across the stony ridges,
  Across the rolling plain,
Young Harry Dale, the drover,
  Comes riding home again.
And well his stock-horse bears him,
  And light of heart is he,
And stoutly his old packhorse
  Is trotting by his knee.

Up Queensland way with cattle
  He travelled regions vast;
And many months have vanished
  Since home-folks saw him last.
He hums a song of someone
  He hopes to marry soon;
And hobble-chains and camp-ware
  Keep jingling to the tune.

Beyond the hazy dado
  Against the lower skies
And yon blue line of ranges
  The station homestead lies.
And thitherward the drover
  Jogs through the lazy noon,
While hobble-chains and camp-ware
  Are jingling to a tune.

An hour has filled the heavens
  With storm-clouds inky black;
At times the lightning trickles
  Around the drover's track;
But Harry pushes onward,
  His horses' strength he tries,
In hope to reach the river
  Before the flood shall rise.

The thunder from above him
  Goes rolling o'er the plain;
And down on thirsty pastures
  In torrents falls the rain.
And every creek and gully
  Sends forth its little flood —
Till the river runs a banker,
  All stained with yellow mud.

Now Harry speaks to Rover,
  The best dog on the plains,
And to his hardy horses,
  And strokes their shaggy manes;
'We've breasted bigger rivers
  When floods were at their height,
Nor shall this gutter stop us
  From getting home to-night!'

The thunder growls a warning,
  The ghastly lightnings gleam,
As the drover turns his horses
  To swim the fatal stream.
But, oh! the flood runs stronger
  Than e'er it ran before;
The saddle-horse is failing,
  And only half-way o'er!

When flashes next the lightning,
  The flood's grey breast is blank,
A cattle-dog and packhorse
  Are struggling up the bank.
But in the lonely homestead
  The girl will wait in vain —
He'll never pass the stations
  In charge of stock again.

The faithful dog a moment
  Lies panting on the bank,
And then swims through the current
  To where his master sank.
And round and round in circles
  He fights with failing strength,
Till, borne down by the waters,
  The old dog sinks at length.

Across the flooded lowlands
  And slopes of sodden loam
The packhorse struggles onward
  To take dumb tidings home.
And mud-stained, wet, and weary,
  Through ranges dark goes he;
While hobble-chains and tinware
  Are sounding eerily.

The floods are in the ocean,
  The stream is clear again,
And now a verdant carpet
  Is stretched across the plain.
But someone's eyes are saddened,
  And someone's heart still bleeds
In sorrow for the drover
  Who sleeps among the reeds.

HENRY LAWSON

The Ballad of the Drover — An appreciation

(1) What are Harry's feelings as the poem opens?
(2) Why is he looking forward to seeing 'someone'?
(3) Apart from the tune he is humming, what sound accompanies him as he rides?

(4)   At what point, and why, does Harry's mood begin to change?

(5)   Why does Harry push on with all speed?

(6)   What is Harry's attitude to the river?

(7)   What happens in the seventh stanza?

(8)   'The girl will wait in vain', we are told. What has happened?

(9)   How does Rover prove his loyalty?

(10)   Who is the sole survivor of the tragedy?

(11)   What word describes the hollow, ghostly way in which the gear on the packhorse resounds in the lonely ranges?

(12)   What is the contrast that is presented in the last stanza?

The next poem depicts a scene which will never be witnessed by Australians again — motor-transport has made the bullock teams obsolete. As you read the poem, picture the struggles and hardships endured by a bullocky and his team.

THE TEAMS

A cloud of dust on the long, white road,
And the teams go creeping on
Inch by inch with the weary load;
And by the power of the green-hide goad
The distant goal is won.

With eyes half-shut to the blinding dust,
And necks to the yokes bent low,
The beasts are pulling as bullocks must;
And the shining tires might almost rust
While the spokes are turning slow.

With face half-hid by a broad-brimmed hat,
That shades from the heat's white waves,
And shouldered whip, with its green-hide plait,
The driver plods with a gait like that
Of his weary, patient slaves.

He wipes his brow, for the day is hot,
And spits to the left with spite;
He shouts at Bally, and flicks at Scot,
And raises dust from the back of Spot,
And spits to the dusty right.

He'll sometimes pause as a thing of form
In front of a settler's door,
And ask for a drink, and remark 'It's warm',
Or say 'There's signs of a thunderstorm';
But he seldom utters more.

The rains are heavy on roads like these
And, fronting his lonely home
For days together the settler sees
The wagons bogged to the axletrees,
Or ploughing the sodden loam.

And then, when the roads are at their worst,
The bushmen's children hear
The cruel blows of the whips reversed
While the bullocks pull as their hearts would burst
And bellow with pain and fear.

And thus — with glimpses of home and rest —
Are the long, long journeys done;
And thus — 'tis a thankless life at the best! —
Is Distance fought in the mighty West,
And the lonely battle won.

HENRY LAWSON

The Teams — Reading for meaning

(1) What distant sign indicated that the teams were on the move?
(2) What does 'inch by inch' suggest about the bullocks' load?
(3) How did the bullocks react to 'the blinding dust'?
(4) Can you find examples of cruelty, hardship and struggle in the poem?
(5) What evidence can you find to suggest that it was extremely hot?
(6) What did the driver do as he plodded along beside his animals?
(7) The rhythm of the poem is slow and measured. Can you suggest why?
(8) What do you think made the driver indifferent (not caring one way or the other) to human comfort and company?
(9) In days of heavy rain, what might a settler see on the road in front of his home?
(10) What sounds did the bushmen's children hear?
(11) The final line in the last stanza picks up and echoes the final line in the first stanza. The 'distant goal' gains more meaning. Explain.

Henry Lawson now describes for us another scene from bygone days. In his travels, Lawson no doubt experienced at first hand some of the hardships referred to in this and the preceding poem.

ANDY'S GONE WITH CATTLE

Our Andy's gone with cattle now —
Our hearts are out of order —
With drought he's gone to battle now
Across the Queensland border.
He's left us in dejection now,
Our thoughts with him are roving;
It's dull on this selection now,
Since Andy went a-droving.

Who now shall wear the cheerful face
In times when things are slackest?
And who shall whistle round the place
When Fortune frowns her blackest?
Oh, who shall cheek the squatter now
When he comes round us snarling?
His tongue is getting hotter now
Since Andy crossed the Darling.

Oh, may the showers in torrents fall
And all the tanks run over;
And may the grass grow green and tall
In pathways of the drover;
And may good angels send the rain
On desert stretches sandy;
And when the summer comes again
God grant 'twill bring us Andy.

HENRY LAWSON

Andy's Gone with Cattle — Some questions

(1) Why did Andy go to Queensland?

(2) 'Our hearts are out of order' is an unusual expression. What does it mean?

(3) What word tells you that drought was regarded as an enemy?

(4) What was it like on the selection when Andy was away? (A selection was a property *selected* from the bush — sometimes not legally!)

(5) What kind of a person was Andy?

(6) Are we told anything about Andy's attitude to the squatter?

(7) 'His tongue is getting hotter now'
Can you explain the meaning of this line?

(8) How do we know from this poem that life was very harsh for those on the land?

Notice, as you read 'The Stockman', how the first stanza sets the scene — the heat, the grass, the trees, the stockman sitting on his heel and making the small movements of rolling a smoke. It's a scene almost out of time — it could have occurred at any point over the past hundred years or so.

In the second stanza, other objects are added to the scene: the horse, the dog and Time, all waiting a while.

In the third stanza, the stockman rides away, but ... in a twist of time ...

THE STOCKMAN

The sun was in the summer grass,
The coolibahs were twisted steel;
The stockman paused beneath their shade
And sat upon his heel,
And with the reins looped through his arm
He rolled tobacco in his palm.

His horse stood still. His cattle dog
Tongued in the shadow of the tree,
And for a moment on the plain
Time waited for the three.
And then the stockman licked his fag
And Time took up his solar swag.

I saw the stockman mount and ride
Across the mirage on the plain;
And still that timeless moment brought
Fresh ripples to my brain:
It seemed in that distorting air
I saw his grandson sitting there.

DAVID CAMPBELL

Here is another picture of a rugged Australian from our past.

NINE MILES FROM GUNDAGAI

I've done my share of shearing sheep,
Of droving and all that,
And bogged a bullock-team as well
  On a Murrumbidgee flat.
I've seen the bullock stretch and strain
And blink his bleary eye,
And the dog sits on the tucker-box
  Nine miles from Gundagai.

I've been jilted, jarred and crossed in love,
And sand-bagged in the dark,
Till, if a mountain fell on me,
  I'd treat it as a lark.
It's when you've got your bullocks bogged,
That's the time you flog and cry,
And the dog sits on the tucker-box
  Nine miles from Gundagai.

JACK MOSES

CLANCY OF THE OVERFLOW

I had written him a letter which I had, for want of better
Knowledge, sent to where I met him down the Lachlan, years ago;
He was shearing when I knew him, so I sent the letter to him
Just on spec, addressed as follows, 'Clancy, of The Overflow'.

And an answer came directed in a writing unexpected
(And I think the same was written with a thumb-nail dipped in tar);
'Twas his shearing mate who wrote it, and verbatim I will quote it:
'Clancy's gone to Queensland droving, and we don't know where he
    are.'

In my wild erratic fancy visions come to me of Clancy
Gone a-droving 'down the Cooper' where the Western drovers go;
As the stock are slowly stringing, Clancy rides behind them singing,
For the drover's life has pleasures that the townsfolk never know.

And the bush has friends to meet him, and their kindly voices greet
    him
In the murmur of the breezes and the river on its bars,
And he sees the vision splendid of the sunlit plains extended,
And at night the wondrous glory of the everlasting stars.

I am sitting in my dingy little office, where a stingy
Ray of sunlight struggles feebly down between the houses tall,
And the foetid air and gritty of the dusty, dirty city
Through the open window floating, spreads its foulness over all.

And in place of lowing cattle, I can hear the fiendish rattle
Of the tramways and the buses making hurry down the street;
And the language uninviting of the gutter children fighting
Comes fitfully and faintly through the ceaseless tramp of feet.

And the hurrying people daunt me, and their pallid faces haunt me
As they shoulder one another in their rush and nervous haste,
With their eager eyes and greedy, and their stunted forms and
    weedy,
For townsfolk have no time to grow, they have no time to waste.

And I somehow rather fancy that I'd like to change with Clancy,
Like to take a turn at droving where the seasons come and go,
While he faced the round eternal of the cash-book and the journal —
    But I doubt he'd suit the office, Clancy of The Overflow.

A. B. ('BANJO') PATERSON

Clancy of the Overflow — For you to consider

(1)   Written 'with a thumb-nail dipped in tar'. Describe the kind of writing that these words call up in your imagination.

(2)   What are the poet's feelings about country life?

(3)   'And the bush has friends to meet him ...'
Who or what are the 'friends'?

(4)   What is 'the vision splendid'?

(5)   What are the poet's feelings about city life?

(6)   What word seems to make you *hear* the sound of the trams and buses out in the street?

(7)   What is the poet's wish at the end of the poem?

(8)   Why does the poet think that this wish could not possibly come true?

(9)   'While he faced the round eternal of the cash-book and the journal —'
Explain this line in your own words.

(10)   What impression does the poet give us of Clancy? What impression does the poet give us of himself?

Discussion Point

This poem is one of the Australian 'greats'. What is there about 'Clancy of the Overflow' that has made it both lasting and popular?

Next, a very appealing little poem about things and surroundings which are snug, comfortable and peaceful. It's also about tried and tested things — things which are more like old friends than like possessions — and the satisfaction they give.

THE OLD BLACK BILLY AN' ME

The sheep are yarded, an' I sit
Beside the fire an' poke at it.
Far from the booze, an' clash o' men,
Glad, I'm glad I'm back again
On the station, wi' me traps,
An' fencing wire, an' tanks an' taps.
Back to salt-bush plains, an' flocks,
An' old bark hut be th' apple-box.
I turn the slipjack, make the tea,
All's as still as still can be —
An' the old black billy winks at me.

LOUIS ESSON

Read this poem aloud and pick up the rhythm of a loping dog.

LONE DOG

I'm a lean dog, a keen dog, a wild dog, and lone;
I'm a rough dog, a tough dog, hunting on my own;
I'm a bad dog, a mad dog, teasing silly sheep;
I love to sit and bay the moon, to keep fat souls from sleep.

I'll never be a lap dog, licking dirty feet,
A sleek dog, a meek dog, cringing for my meat,
Not for me the fireside, the well-filled plate,
But shut door, and sharp stone, and cuff, and kick, and hate.

Not for me the other dogs, running by my side,
Some have run a short while, but none of them would bide,
O mine is still the lone trail, the hard trail, the best,
Wild wind, and wild stars, and the hunger of the quest!

IRENE R. McLEOD

THE MAN FROM SNOWY RIVER

There was movement at the station, for the word had passed around
   That the colt from old Regret had got away,
And had joined the wild bush horses — he was worth a thousand
   pound,
   So all the cracks had gathered to the fray.
All the tried and noted riders from the stations near and far
   Had mustered at the homestead overnight,
For the bushmen love hard riding where the wild bush horses are,
   And the stock-horse snuffs the battle with delight.

There was Harrison, who made his pile when Pardon won the cup,
   The old man with his hair as white as snow;
But few could ride beside him when his blood was fairly up —
   He would go wherever horse and man could go.
And Clancy of the Overflow came down to lend a hand,
   No better horseman ever held the reins;
For never horse could throw him while the saddle-girths would
   stand,
   He learnt to ride while droving on the plains.

And one was there, a stripling on a small and weedy beast;
   He was something like a racehorse undersized,
With a touch of Timor pony — three parts thoroughbred at least —
   And such as are by mountain horsemen prized.
He was hard and tough and wiry — just the sort that won't say
     die —
   There was courage in his quick impatient tread;
And he bore the badge of gameness in his bright and fiery eye,
   And the proud and lofty carriage of his head.

But still so slight and weedy, one would doubt his power to stay,
   And the old man said, 'That horse will never do
For a long and tiring gallop — lad, you'd better stop away,
   Those hills are far too rough for such as you.'
So he waited, sad and wistful — only Clancy stood his friend —
   'I think we ought to let him come,' he said.
'I warrant he'll be with us when he's wanted at the end,
   For both his horse and he are mountain bred.

'He hails from Snowy River, up by Kosciusko's side,
   Where the hills are twice as steep and twice as rough;
Where a horse's hoofs strike firelight from the flint-stones every
     stride,
   The man that holds his own is good enough.
And the Snowy River riders on the mountains make their home,
   Where the river runs those giant hills between;
I have seen full many horsemen since I first commenced to roam,
   But nowhere yet such horsemen have I seen.'

So he went; they found the horses by the big mimosa clump,
   They raced away towards the mountain's brow,
And the old man give his orders, 'Boys, go at them from the jump,
   No use to try for fancy riding now.
And, Clancy, you must wheel them, try and wheel them to the
     right.
   Ride boldly, lad, and never fear the spills,
For never yet was rider that could keep the mob in sight,
   If once they gain the shelter of those hills.'

So Clancy rode to wheel them — he was racing on the wing
  Where the best and boldest riders take their place,
And he raced his stock-horse past them, and he made the ranges
    ring
  With the stockwhip, as he met them face to face.
Then they halted for a moment, while he swung the dreaded lash,
  But they saw their well-loved mountain full in view,
And they charged beneath the stockwhip with a sharp and sudden
    dash,
  And off into the mountain scrub they flew.

Then fast the horsemen followed, where the gorges deep and black
  Resounded to the thunder of their tread,
And the stockwhips woke the echoes, and they fiercely answered
    back
  From cliffs and crags that beetled overhead.
And upward, ever upward, the wild horses held their way,
  Where mountain ash and kurrajong grew wide;
And the old man muttered fiercely, 'We may bid the mob good day,
  No man can hold them down the other side.'

When they reached the mountain's summit, even Clancy took a pull —
  It well might make the boldest hold their breath;
The wild hop scrub grew thickly, and the hidden ground was full
  Of wombat holes, and any slip was death.
But the Man from Snowy River let the pony have his head,
  And he swung his stockwhip round and gave a cheer,
And he raced him down the mountain like a torrent down its bed,
  While the others stood and watched in very fear.

He sent the flint-stones flying, but the pony kept his feet,
  He cleared the fallen timber in his stride,
And the Man from Snowy River never shifted in his seat —
  It was grand to see that mountain horseman ride.
Through the stringy-barks and saplings, on the rough and broken
    ground,
  Down the hillside at a racing pace he went;
And he never drew the bridle till he landed safe and sound
  At the bottom of that terrible descent.

He was right among the horses as they climbed the farther hill,
   And the watchers on the mountain, standing mute,
Saw him ply the stockwhip fiercely; he was right among them still,
   As he raced across the clearing in pursuit.
Then they lost him for a moment, where two mountain gullies met
   In the ranges — but a final glimpse reveals
On a dim and distant hillside the wild horses racing yet,
   With the Man from Snowy River at their heels.

And he ran them single-handed till their sides were white with
     foam;
   He followed like a bloodhound on their track,
Till they halted, cowed and beaten; then he turned their heads for
     home,
   And alone and unassisted brought them back.
But his hardy mountain pony he could scarcely raise a trot,
   He was blood from hip to shoulder from the spur;
But his pluck was still undaunted, and his courage fiery hot,
   For never yet was mountain horse a cur.

And down by Kosciusko, where the pine-clad ridges raise
   Their torn and rugged battlements on high,
Where the air is clear as crystal, and the white stars fairly blaze
   At midnight in the cold and frosty sky,
And where around the Overflow the reed-beds sweep and sway
   To the breezes, and the rolling plains are wide,
The Man from Snowy River is a household word to-day,
   And the stockmen tell the story of his ride.

A. B. PATERSON

The Man from Snowy River — Looking closely

(1) Why was old Regret's colt worth chasing?

(2) Explain in your own words, 'So all the cracks had gathered to the fray'.

(3) The loss of the colt was not exactly a tragedy for either the bushmen or their horses. Why not?

(4) Harrison was a wealthy old man. How did he make his fortune?

(5) What kind of reputation did Clancy of the Overflow have as a horseman?

(6) Although the stripling owned only 'a small and weedy beast', it was both courageous and game. What signs in the pony suggested this?

(7) Nobody wanted the lad and his pony to go on the chase — except Clancy. Why did Clancy believe in him?

(8) Find a line from Clancy's description of the Snowy country (5th stanza) that explains why the Snowy horsemen have to be exceptional.

(9) In the plan to catch the wild bush-horses, Clancy's job was to wheel the mob to the right. What did this move aim to prevent?

(10) What two sounds are given strong emphasis as the horsemen chase the mob into the gorges?

(11)   'Through the stringy-barks and saplings, on the rough and broken
        ground . . .'
        This line isn't an easy line to say. The words are spiky and uneven.
        Can you suggest why it might have been written this way?

(12)   The last stanza is different from the others
        (i) in time, and
        (ii) in what it talks about.
        Can you give more details? Why did the poet write it this way?

(13)   The rhythm in the poem often has a racy, pounding beat. Can you
        say why?

Discussion Point

The qualities of courage, skill and endurance shown in this poem are
still present and still needed in Australia today. Do you agree?

---

2. Similes and Metaphors

The poet works with words, often putting them together so skilfully that they call up pictures in our minds. Such patterns of picture-giving words are called **figures of speech**.

Two figures of speech that are commonly used to put us in the picture are the SIMILE and the METAPHOR. Let's take each in turn.

Similes

The simile asks us to picture one thing as being similar to another — often using the word 'like' or the words 'as ... as' to link our 'pictures' in the mind.

Examples:

She swims   like a   fish.   He's as hairy   as a   gorilla.

Get the picture? Good. Now try this exercise:

Similes are pictured below and overleaf. Supply the missing words.

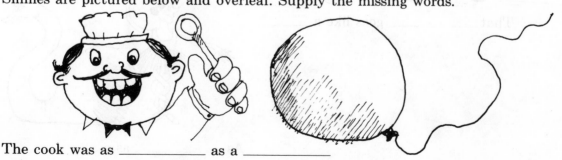

The cook was as _____ as a _____

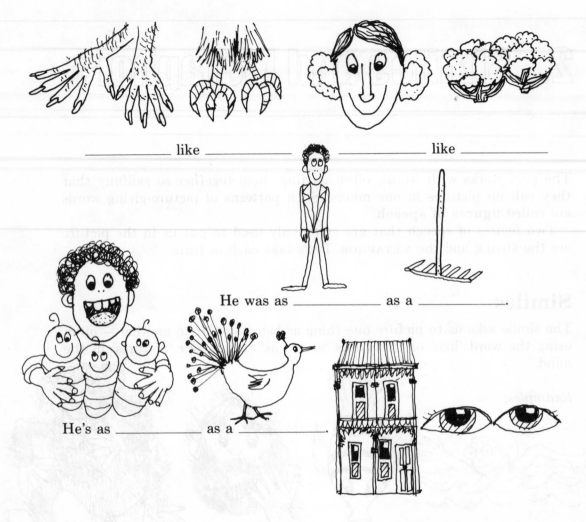

_____ like _____   _____ like _____

He was as _____ as a _____.

He's as _____ as a _____.

The _____ were like _____.

That _____ goes like a _____.

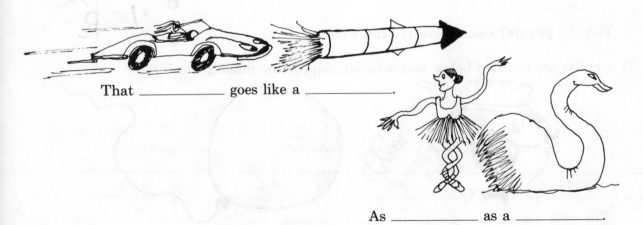

As _____ as a _____.

Simile Practice

There are many familiar similes in which comparisons are made with (a) animals and birds, and (b) things or objects.

Using the boxes, complete the similes by filling in (a) the animals or birds, and (b) the things or objects.

ANIMALS & BIRDS

monkeys	leech	owl	lamb	mule
lark	hyena	ox	wolf	ostrich
elephants	coot	hawk	sheep	duck

(1)   He laughs like a ....
(2)   She's as hungry as a ....
(3)   He waddled like a ....
(4)   He's as bald as a ....
(5)   She was as gentle as a ....
(6)   The crowds poured into the oval like .... into a paddock.
(7)   She's as wise as an ....
(8)   He clung like a .... to his surfboard.
(9)   He's as strong as an ....
(10) She wouldn't listen, she was like an .... with its head in the sand.
(11) She was as happy as a ....
(12) The players lumbered like .... through the mud to the finishing line.
(13) She had eyes like a ....
(14) They clung to the tree's branches, as agile as ....
(15) She's as obstinate as a ....

THINGS/OBJECTS

berries	ABC	arrow	lead	whip
leaf	wind	ghost	honey	silk	thieves
feather	mustard	hammer	furnace	

(1) It was as heavy as ....
(2) You look as white as a ....
(3) The sprinters ran like the ....
(4) With a fist like a .... he pounded the desk.
(5) They're as keen as ....
(6) She's as sweet as ....
(7) They've been out in the sun all day and now they're as brown as
     ....
(8) She's as light as a ....
(9) His voice cracked out like a ....
(10) As straight as an ...., the road ran from the coast to the
     hills.
(11) He was so cold that he was trembling like a ....
(12) Allow me, it's as easy as ....
(13) Out beyond the shade, it's as hot as a ....
(14) It's as smooth as ....
(15) They're as thick as ....

A Simile Poem

Here is a poem about a greyhound. Read it through to yourself.

HOW A GOOD GREYHOUND IS SHAPED

A head like a snake, a neck like a drake,
A back like a beam, a belly like a bream,
A foot like a cat, a tail like a rat.

ANONYMOUS

Did you notice that it was completely made up of similes? Now try to write an animal poem of your own, also made up of similes. You may like to use the following model to write your simile poem.

HOW A GOOD .... IS SHAPED

A head like a ...., a neck like a ....
A nose like a ...., a mouth like a ....
An ear like a ...., a body like a ....

A great deal of good fun can be had by writing simile poems about people you know. Try some and read them aloud to the class, without revealing the names of the persons you write about.

Metaphors

The metaphor goes a step further than the simile and instead of asking us to picture one thing as *being like* another, we are asked to picture one thing as *being* (or 'merging with') another.

Example: Have you ever thought, looking up at the sky, that the moon moving through the clouds looked rather like a ship sailing through the heavy seas? The idea is pictured in this simile:

The moon was like a ghostly galleon tossed upon cloudy seas.

But the metaphor goes a step further and *merges* the two pictures:

The moon was a ghostly galleon tossed upon cloudy seas.

Two Metaphor Poems

Here is a very unusual poem. It is a metaphor, a rather long one, in which Jane takes on the appearance and habits of a bird.

MY SISTER JANE

And I say nothing — no, not a word
About our Jane. Haven't you heard?
She's a bird, a bird, a bird, a bird.
Oh it never would do to let folks know
My sister's nothing but a great big crow.

Each day (we daren't send her to school)
She pulls on stockings of thick blue wool
To make her pin crow legs look right,
Then fits a wig of curls on tight,
And dark spectacles — a huge pair
To cover her very crowy stare.
Oh it never would do to let folks know
My sister's nothing but a great big crow.

When visitors come she sits upright
(With her wings and her tail tucked out of sight).
They think her queer but extremely polite.
Then when the visitors have gone
She whips out her wings and with her wig on
Whirls through the house at the height of your head —
Duck, duck, or she'll knock you dead.
Oh it never would do to let folks know
My sister's nothing but a great big crow.

At meals whatever she sees she'll stab it —
Because she's a crow and that's a crow habit.
My mother says 'Jane! Your manners! Please!'
Then she'll sit quietly on the cheese,
Or play the piano nicely by dancing on the keys —
Oh it never would do to let folks know
My sister's nothing but a great big crow.

TED HUGHES

My Sister Jane — A bird or a Jane?

(1)　Try to draw a picture of Jane as the poet has described her.

(2)　What parts of Jane's body are similar to those of a crow?

(3)　What are some of the things that Jane does which, metaphorically speaking, make her a crow?

(4)　Do you think that by using a metaphor of a bird to describe Jane, the poet is being cruel in any way?

(5)　In what ways do you think the poet could be exaggerating in his description of Jane?

You'll see that the subject of the following poem is — a poem! The whole of 'How to Eat a Poem' is a startling metaphor. Read it and find out what the metaphor is.

HOW TO EAT A POEM

Don't be polite.
Bite in.
Pick it up with your fingers and lick the juice that
　　may run down your chin.
It is ready and ripe now, whenever you are.

You do not need a knife or fork or spoon
or plate or napkin or tablecloth.

For there is no core
or stem
or rind
or pit
or seed
or skin
to throw away.

EVE MERRIAM

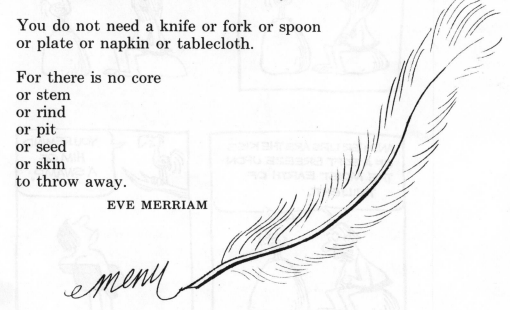

Metaphors in the Comic Strips

Metaphors can be found in all types of writing — even in comic strips and cartoons! See how easily you can identify the metaphors in the following comic strips.

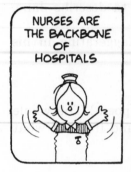

"A bit of a wet blanket, is he? Better invite him anyhow. With the bushfire season just starting, he might come in handy!"

A Mixture of Similes and Metaphors

Here's a poem, 'Concrete Mixers', with a good mixture of similes and metaphors. Copy the poem into your books. Put a single line under the similes and a double line under the metaphors. Then draw the concrete mixers as they are described in the poem.

CONCRETE MIXERS

The drivers are washing the concrete mixers;
Like elephant tenders they hose them down.
Tough grey-skinned monsters standing ponderous,
Elephant-bellied and elephant-nosed,
Standing in muck up to their wheel-caps,
Like rows of elephants, tail to trunk.
Their drivers perch on their backs like mahouts,
Sending the sprays of water up.
They rid the trunk-like trough of concrete,
Direct the spray to the bulging sides,
Turn and start the monsters moving.
   Concrete mixers
   Move like elephants
   Bellow like elephants
   Spray like elephants,
Concrete mixers are urban elephants,
Their trunks are raising a city.

PATRICIA HUBBELL

Simile or Metaphor?

Decide which of the following expressions are similes and which are metaphors. A good way of doing this is to draw up two columns in your book, headed SIMILES and METAPHORS, and then simply to write each of the expressions under one or other of the headings.

(1)   Her eyes they shone like diamonds.
(2)   The moon's a balloon
(3)   Suddenly she arched her back like a horseshoe.
(4)   Silver-hatted mushrooms
(5)   At the end of the street lives small Miss Wing,
        A feathery, fluttery bird of a thing.
(6)   The truck flew down the empty highway.
(7)   Your ears pop like champagne corks.
(8)   His eyes peer from his hair and beard like mice from a load of hay.
(9)   The sea is a mirror for the clouds.
(10) The shadows were as black as sin.
(11) The wind was a whip that cracked over our heads.
(12) I have seen old ships sail like swans asleep.
(13) He's as wild as a dingo.
(14) The stars are pinpricks in the velvet of the night sky.
(15) She came — and then, ghost-like, vanished.
(16) Enthusiasm is your key to success.
(17) She's as pretty as a picture.
(18) Watch out — it's that bullet-headed man again!
(19) They were as quiet as mice.
(20) Teeth like pearls
(21) The road arrowed into the hills.
(22) Education is your passport to satisfying employment.

3. People

THE POSTMAN

Satchel on hip
the postman goes
from doorstep to doorstep
and stooping sows

each letterbox
with seed. His right
hand all the morning makes
the same half circle. White

seed he scatters,
a fistful of
featureless letters
pregnant with ruin or love.

I watch him zig-
zag down the street
dipping his hand in that big
bag, sowing the cool, neat

envelopes which
make *twenty-one*
unaccountably rich,
twenty-two an orphan.

I cannot see
them but I know
others are watching. We
stoop in a row

(as he turns away),
straighten and stand
weighing and delaying
the future in one hand.

JON STALLWORTHY

The Postman — Explanations required

(1)   Explain what is meant by 'sows each letterbox with seed'. What is this figure of speech called?

(2)   How is it that the letters can be described as 'featureless'?

(3)   How can a letter be 'pregnant with ruin or love'?

(4)   What are 'twenty-one' and 'twenty-two'? Why are they in italic type?

(5)   What feature of letters is being emphasised in the stanza which begins, 'envelopes which . . .'?

(6)   What are the various persons doing when they 'stand weighing and delaying the future in one hand'?

(7)   What is the effect of the short, broken lines? Do they contribute in any way to our view of the subject of this poem?

Inventors sometimes seem a little crazy!

Here's an inventor who's a little different — Uncle Dan!

UNCLE DAN

My Uncle Dan's an inventor, you may think that's very fine,
You may wish he was your Uncle instead of being mine —
If he wanted he could make a watch that bounces when it drops,
He could make a helicopter out of string and bottle tops
Or any really useful thing you can't get in the shops.

    But Uncle Dan has other ideas:
    The bottomless glass for ginger beers,
    The toothless saw that's safe for the tree,
    A special word for a spelling bee
    (Like Lionocerangoutangadder),
    Or the roll-uppable rubber ladder,
    The mystery pie that bites when it's bit —
    My Uncle Dan invented it.

My Uncle Dan sits in his den inventing night and day.
His eyes peer from his hair and beard like mice from a load of hay.
And does he make the shoes that will go walks without your feet?
A shrinker to shrink instantly the elephants you meet?
A carver that just carves from the air steaks cooked and ready to
      eat?

    No, no, he has other intentions —
    Only perfectly useless inventions:
    Glassless windows (they never break)
    A medicine to cure the earthquake
    The unspillable screwed-down cup,
    The stairs that go neither down nor up,
    The door you simply paint on a wall —
    Uncle Dan invented them all.

                          TED HUGHES

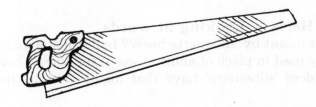

SILHOUETTE HEELS

I have me a place which is all me own
When me old man dags me
    and me mother — she can't stop her moan
I put on me silhouette heels and go
    clicking down the stairs.

At the bus stop I pay me fare — one (sh) and six (d)
And I go find me a seat at the top
Where the wind changes me from a dumb sheila
    with good legs to *someone*.
My mind is free to think and dream;
I become a princess, Sophia Loren, the Queen;
    — not myself.

Suddenly the bus stops — I get off and walk through
    the town
And I can't help myself from wiggling and noticing
    all the eyes on me
And if there's a 'nicee' I might give him a 'come-on'.
I drop in at the pub and have me a few
But soon it's time for me, again, to get home.

Again I pay me one and six and sit in the top — my
    special place
where I can wish, dream, I was someone.

I get off at my stop
And go clicking up the stairs in my silhouette heels
Me old man will dag me
    and me mother won't stop her moan;
And maybe again I'll go to me special place —
    to dream, to wish . . .

                IRENE KOLTUNIEWICZ

Silhouette Heels — Looking at words

(1)   What is meant by 'silhouette heels'? Is this just a malapropism (a word wrongly used in place of another word) for *stiletto* heels? What associations does 'silhouette' have that might also fit the subject of this poem?

(2) What do you think 'dags' means? Is it all right to use slang like this in a poem? What guidelines would you offer to someone who asked when it was correct to use slang and when it wasn't?

(3) What are some of the things that happen in the girl's imagination when she 'becomes a princess'?

(4) What is meant by a 'nicee' and what is a 'come-on'?

(5) Suggest an explanation for the fact that the girl sometimes uses 'me' ('me mother') and sometimes uses 'my' ('my special place').

(6) What does the language suggest to *you* about this girl?

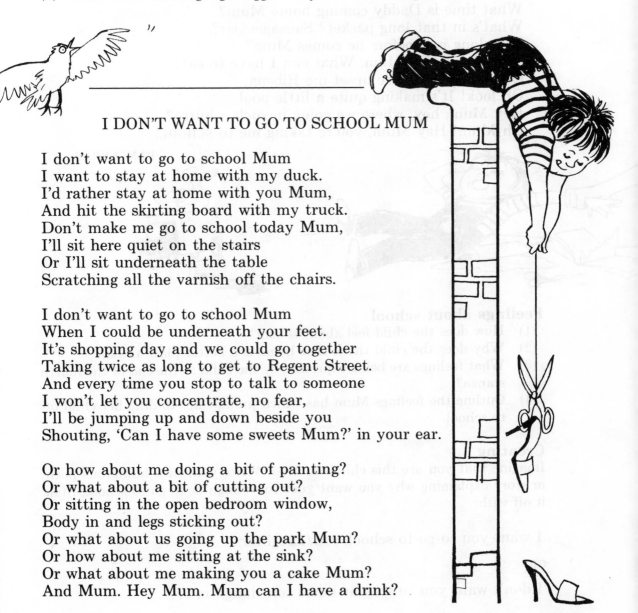

I DON'T WANT TO GO TO SCHOOL MUM

I don't want to go to school Mum
I want to stay at home with my duck.
I'd rather stay at home with you Mum,
And hit the skirting board with my truck.
Don't make me go to school today Mum,
I'll sit here quiet on the stairs
Or I'll sit underneath the table
Scratching all the varnish off the chairs.

I don't want to go to school Mum
When I could be underneath your feet.
It's shopping day and we could go together
Taking twice as long to get to Regent Street.
And every time you stop to talk to someone
I won't let you concentrate, no fear,
I'll be jumping up and down beside you
Shouting, 'Can I have some sweets Mum?' in your ear.

Or how about me doing a bit of painting?
Or what about a bit of cutting out?
Or sitting in the open bedroom window,
Body in and legs sticking out?
Or what about us going up the park Mum?
Or how about me sitting at the sink?
Or what about me making you a cake Mum?
And Mum. Hey Mum. Mum can I have a drink?

And Mum, Mum what's that at the bottom of the cupboard?
And Mum, what's in the bag you put down there?
And hey Mum watch me jump straight off the sofa,
And Mum, whose dog is that stood over there?
What you doing Mum? Peeling potatoes?
Sit me on the drainer watching you
I wouldn't *mind* me trousers getting wet Mum.
Oh I aren't half fed up. What can I do?

What time is Daddy coming home Mum?
What's in that long packet? Sausagemeat?
How long is it before he comes Mum?
And Mum. Hey Mum. What can I have to eat?
Oh sorry Mum! I've upset me Ribena.
Oh look! It's making quite a little pool.
Hey Mum, hey, where we going in such a hurry?
Oh Mum! Hey Mum, you're taking me to SCHOOL!

PAM AYRES

Feelings about school

(1) How does the child feel about school?
(2) Why does the child think that home is a better place to be?
(3) What feelings are being expressed by the child at the end of the fourth stanza?
(4) Outline the feelings Mum has which prompt her to drag her child off to school.

Creating

Imagine that you are this child's mother. Write your own humorous poem or story explaining why you want your son/daughter to go to school. Start it off with:

'I want you to go to school, son/daughter ...'

OR

'I don't want you to stay at home son/daughter ..'

AFRICAN BEGGAR

Sprawled in the dust outside the Syrian store,
a target for small children, dogs and flies,
a heap of verminous rags and matted hair,
he watches us with cunning, reptile eyes,
his noiseless, smallpoxed face creased in a sneer.

Sometimes he shows his yellow stumps of teeth
and whines for alms, perceiving that we bear
the curse of pity; a grotesque mask of death,
with hands like claws about his begging-bowl.

But often he is lying all alone
within the shadow of a crumbling wall,
lost in the trackless jungle of his pain,
clutching the pitiless red earth in vain
and whimpering like a stricken animal.

RAYMOND TONG

African Beggar — Emotions

(1) Which of the following words do you feel comes closest to describing the poet's emotions?

**sympathy, anger, revulsion, dislike,
irritation, compassion, detachment, pity**

(2) Now try to find evidence in the poem to support your choice in the question above.

(3) What would your own feelings have been towards this beggar?

This narrative poem from early last century records the daring abduction of Ellen by the young Scottish lord, Lochinvar. The strong lively rhythm of the poem and the appeal of its exciting and romantic theme have made it popular with all generations since.

LOCHINVAR

O, young Lochinvar is come out of the west,
Through all the wide Border[1] his steed was the best;
And save his good broadsword he weapons had none,
He rode all unarm'd and he rode all alone.
So faithful in love and so dauntless in war,
There never was knight like the young Lochinvar.

He staid not for brake, and he stopp'd not for stone,
He swam the Eske river where ford there was none;
But ere he alighted at Netherby gate,
The bride had consented,[2] the gallant came late:
For a laggard in love, and a dastard in war
Was to wed the fair Ellen of brave Lochinvar.

So boldly he enter'd the Netherby Hall,
Among the bride's-men, and kinsmen, and brothers, and all:
Then spoke the bride's father, his hand on his sword
(For the poor craven bridegroom said never a word)
'O come ye in peace here, or come ye in war,
Or to dance at our bridal, young Lord Lochinvar?'

'I long woo'd your daughter, my suit you denied;
Love swells like the Solway, but ebbs like the tide —
And now am I come, with this lost love of mine,
To lead but one measure, drink one cup of wine.
There are maidens in Scotland more lovely by far,
That would gladly be bride to the young Lochinvar.'

The bride kiss'd the goblet: the knight took it up.
He quaff'd off the wine, and he threw down the cup.
She look'd down to blush, and she look'd up to sigh,
With a smile on her lips, and a tear in her eye.
He took her soft hand, ere her mother could bar —
'Now tread we a measure!' said young Lochinvar.

1 *Border:* The country around the border between England and Scotland.
2 *had consented:* i.e. to marry somebody else.

So stately his form, and so lovely her face,
That never a hall such a galliard³ did grace;
While her mother did fret, and her father did fume,
And the bridegroom stood dangling his bonnet and plume;
And the bride-maidens whisper'd, "Twere better by far,
To have matched our fair cousin with young Lochinvar.'

One touch to her hand, and one word in her ear,
When they reach'd the hall-door, and the charger stood near;
So light to the croupe⁴ the fair lady he swung,
So light to the saddle before her he sprung!
'She is won! we are gone, over bank, bush, and scaur;
They'll have fleet steeds that follow,' quoth young Lochinvar.

There was mounting 'mong Graemes of the Netherby clan;
Forsters, Fenwicks, and Musgraves, they rode and they ran;
There was racing and chasing on Cannobie Lee,
But the lost bride of Netherby ne'er did they see.
So daring in love, and so dauntless in war,
Have ye e'er heard a gallant like young Lochinvar?

SIR WALTER SCOTT

3 *galliard:* a type of dance.
4 *croupe:* place behind the saddle.

Lochinvar — Finding the clues

(1) What clues can you find to suggest that Lochinvar was (a) fearless, and (b) determined?
(2) What clues show that Ellen really loved Lochinvar?
(3) What clues can you find that they had been prevented from marrying?
(4) What clues show that Lochinvar had deliberately set out to deceive Ellen's father? Do you think Lochinvar was justified in doing what he did? Give your reasons.
(5) What clues reveal that the bridegroom was cowardly?
(6) What clues tell us that the fair Ellen agreed to go along with Lochinvar?
(7) What clues inform us that Ellen and Lochinvar made a very handsome couple on the dance floor?
(8) What clues show that Ellen's mother and father were worried by Lochinvar's dancing with Ellen?
(9) What clues indicate that Lochinvar had prepared to make a quick exit?
(10) What clues can you find that Ellen's relatives were determined to pursue Lochinvar?

MY BUS CONDUCTOR

My bus conductor tells me
he only has one kidney
and that may soon go on strike
through overwork.
Each bus ticket
takes on now a different shape
and texture.
He holds a ninepenny single
as if it were a rose
and puts the shilling in his bag
as a child into a gasmeter.

His thin lips
have no quips
for fat factory girls
and he ignores
the drunk who snores
and the old man who talks to himself
and gets off at the wrong stop.
He goes gently to the bedroom
of the bus
to collect
and watch familiar shops and pubs pass by
(perhaps for the last time?).
The same old streets look different now
more distinct
as through new glasses.
And the sky
Was it ever so blue?

And all the time
deep down in the deserted bus shelter of his mind
he thinks about his journey nearly done.
One day he'll clock on and never clock off
or clock off and never clock on.

ROGER MCGOUGH

My Bus Conductor — Understanding and responding

(1) What is meant by 'one kidney ... may soon go on strike through overwork'?
(2) What evidence can you find to show that the bus conductor is a changed man?
(3) Explain how a child would put a coin into a gasmeter. What does this image convey about the way the conductor handles the fares now?
(4) What has changed this bus conductor so much?
(5) What is the 'journey' to which his mind constantly returns?
(6) How effectively has the poet created a mood for you in this poem? What is this mood, and what feelings have been aroused?

Sometimes a little humour can hide some fairly strong feelings. In the following poem, how does the poet *really* feel about his former bank manager? The word 'former' is a clue, telling us ... what?

A CURSE ON MY FORMER BANK MANAGER

May your computer twitch every time it remembers money
until the twitches mount and become a mechanical ache
and may the ache increase until the tapes begin to scream
and may the pus of data burst from its metal skin

and just before the downpour of molten aluminium
may you be preening in front of your computer
and may you be saying to your favourite millionaire
yes it cost nine hundred thousand but it repays every penny

and may the hundred-mile tape which records my debts spring out
like a supersonic two-dimensional boa-constrictor
and may it slip under your faultless collar and surround your
    hairless neck
and may it tighten and tighten until it has repaid everything
    I owe you

ADRIAN MITCHELL

Two curses

(1) What do you imagine to be the incident behind this poem? What has the bank manager done to annoy the poet?
(2) Imagine that you have just tried to trade-in your second-hand car on a new one, and that the salesman offered what you consider a pathetic deal. Write a poem or story titled, 'A Curse on a Car Salesman'.

A *tall story* is one in which the exaggeration is so outrageous that it makes you want to laugh. Well, exaggeration goes wild in this poem.

MUMMY SLEPT LATE AND
DADDY FIXED BREAKFAST

Daddy fixed breakfast.
He made us each a waffle.
It looked like gravel pudding.
It tasted something awful.

'Ha, ha,' he said, 'I'll try again.
This time I'll get it right.'
But what *I* got was in between
Bituminous and anthracite.[1]

'A little too well done? Oh well,
I'll have to start all over.'
That time what landed on my plate
Looked like a manhole cover.

I tried to cut it with a fork:
The fork gave off a spark.
I tried a knife and twisted it
Into a question mark.

I tried it with a hack-saw.
I tried it with a torch.
It didn't even make a dent.
It didn't even scorch.

The next time Dad gets breakfast
When Mummy's sleeping late,
I think I'll skip the waffles.
I'd sooner eat the plate!

JOHN CIARDI

1 *bituminous and anthracite:* i.e. soft and hard coal.

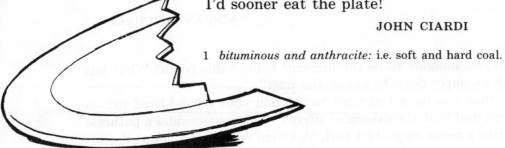

THE SLAVE'S DREAM

Beside the ungathered rice he lay,
　His sickle in his hand;
His breast was bare, his matted hair
　Was buried in the sand.
Again, in the mist and shadow of sleep,
　He saw his Native Land.

Wide through the landscape of his dreams
　The lordly Niger flowed:
Beneath the palm-trees on the plain
　Once more a king he strode;
And heard the tinkling caravans
　Descend the mountain-road.

He saw once more his dark-eyed queen
　Among her children stand;
They clasped his neck, they kissed his cheeks,
　They held him by the hand! —
A tear burst from the sleeper's lids,
　And fell into the sand.

And then at furious speed he rode
　Along the Niger's bank;
His bridle-reins were golden chains,
　And, with a martial clank,
At each leap he could feel his scabbard of steel
　Smiting his stallion's flank.

Before him, like a blood-red flag,
　The bright flamingoes flew;
From morn till night he followed their flight,
　O'er the plains where the tamarind grew,
Till he saw the roofs of Caffre huts,
　And the ocean rose to view.

At night he heard the lion roar,
　And the hyena scream,
And the river-horse, as he crushed the reeds
　Beside some hidden stream;
And it passed, like a glorious roll of drums,
　Through the triumph of his dream.

The forests, with their myriad tongues,
    Shouted of liberty;
And the Blast of the Desert cried aloud,
    With a voice so wild and free,
That he started in his sleep and smiled
    At their tempestuous glee.

He did not feel the driver's whip,
    Nor the burning heat of day;
For Death had illumined the Land of Sleep,
    And his lifeless body lay
A worn-out fetter, that the soul
    Had broken and thrown away!

                    HENRY WADSWORTH LONGFELLOW

The Slave's Dream — Thinking it over
 (1)   What is there at the start of the poem to suggest that the slave still
       has work to do?
 (2)   In former years, what position had this slave held?
 (3)   Identify at least two visible reactions that you might have seen in the
       sleeping slave had you been watching him.
 (4)   Explain why the flamingoes were 'like a blood-red flag'.
 (5)   Identify three animals native to the slave's homeland.
 (6)   Explain what is meant by
           'The forests, with their myriad tongues,
           Shouted of liberty;'
 (7)   What happens to the slave at the end of the poem?
 (8)   Write down your reaction to this poem, explaining why you like or
       dislike it.

This is a very sad poem about poor Butch Weldy. As well as being sad it
shows that, in life, justice is not always on the side of the innocent.

BUTCH WELDY

After I got religion and steadied down
They gave me a job in the canning works,
And every morning I had to fill
The tank in the yard with gasoline,
That fed the blow-fires in the sheds
To heat the soldering irons.

And I mounted a rickety ladder to do it,
Carrying buckets full of the stuff.
One morning, as I stood there pouring,
The air grew still and seemed to heave,
And I shot up as the tank exploded,
And down I came with both legs broken,
And my eyes burned crisp as a couple of eggs.
For someone left a blow-fire going,
And something sucked the flame in the tank.
The Circuit Judge said whoever did it
Was a fellow-servant of mine, and so
Old Rhodes' son didn't have to pay me.
And I sat on the witness stand as blind
As Jack the Fiddler, saying over and over,
'I didn't know him at all.'

EDGAR LEE MASTERS

Butch Weldy — Talking points

(1) Did you agree with the judge's decision that Old Rhodes' son didn't have to pay Butch? Why?
(2) Can you explain why Butch kept saying over and over, 'I didn't know him at all'?
(3) Do you think belonging to a union could have helped Butch?
(4) Have you encountered a lack of justice at school or somewhere else? Give details to the class.
(5) Have you encountered stupid regulations, rules or laws? Describe one of them to the class.

It isn't always possessions and status that make a man a prince. Often, a person's actions are what really counts.

A PRINCE OF MEN

I drove today behind a garbage truck,
Not a modern one — an open one.
In all the waste,
Holding firmly to the upright side
Of one wall of the truck,
A Negro worker stood.
Cold, dripping rain splattered

All around him, all over him.
His clothes were soggy,
Soaked through.
No raincoat. No rainhat.
Only a ragged cap,
A blob of soggy cloth upon his head.
Yet, he was concerned for me.
He noticed that the truck was slowing
My progress;
My progress in the new car,
Warmly heated from the buzzing heater,
Sheltered by the shiny roof above.
He smiled and looked ahead
To see if I could pass
And waved the friendliest wave
To say, 'It's okay. There's no one coming.
    Go on! Pass! Sorry to hold you up!'
As I passed, I wondered.
Would I have cared if anyone was slowed up
In that shiny, heated car?
What prince of men was this?
How did he learn such kindness —
From waste and rain and coldness ... from
Other men?
Would I have waved ... or spit?

JACK NOFFSINGER

A Prince of Men — Understanding
(1)   What is there about the Negro to suggest that he is of a fairly low
       social status?
(2)   How does the poet's position contrast with that of the Negro?
(3)   What makes the poet call the Negro a 'prince of men'?
(4)   The poet is left asking two questions after this incident. What are
       they?

Appreciating
(5)   How does the description of the Negro, starting with 'Cold, dripping
       rain ...', make you feel about this man?
(6)   How successfully does the poet convey to you the impact that this
       incident had on him?
(7)   What is there about this poem that makes you feel it is successful
       or unsuccessful?

4. Sound-Words

There are many words in English that actually suggest the sound of the action they are referring to. Words such as *growl, purr, moo, crunch, squelch, drip, flop, bang, slurp* and *thud* are just a few of the many sound-words we come across every day. The formal name for this occurrence is **onomatopoeia**. Poets use sound-words more than most people. Can you suggest why? Read through the poem 'Company Manners'. Most of the lines contain sound-words.

COMPANY MANNERS

Hands off the tablecloth
don't rumble belly
don't grab for grub
don't slurp the soup
don't crumble the crackers
don't mash the mushrooms
don't mush the potatoes
don't stab the steak
don't slap the saltshaker
don't pill the bread
don't swill the sauce
don't ooze the mayonnaise
don't slop the slaw
don't spatter the ketchup
don't gulp the olives
don't spit the pits
don't finger the lettuce
don't dribble the dressing
don't chomp the celery
don't gobble the cobbler
don't guzzle the fizz
swallow don't swig
don't smack your lips
pat with a napkin
daintily dab
quietly quaff
fastidious sip
and gracefully sample
a nibbling tidbit.

EVE MERRIAM

Do the sound-words in this poem remind you of the sounds heard at the table while people are eating? Pick out two or three of the sound-words which you think are particularly suitable and explain why.

Sound-Words in the Comic Strips

If you look through the comic strips in your local papers you'll find that cartoonists often use onomatopoeic words or sound-words. There is a very good reason for this. The cartoonist, like the poet, is trying to give his pictures life, and also to say as much as possible in a limited space. Now read through these comic strips and see whether you can answer the questions concerning the sound-words.

ST PIPS —   By Neil Matterson

I HAVE TO ADMIRE MATRON'S ABILITY TO CONTROL AN UNRULY PATIENT

SHE COMBINES HER PROFESSIONAL COOLNESS WITH YEARS OF EXPERIENCE AND ABILITY

BIFF

NOT FORGETTING 99% BRUTE STRENGTH!

FRED BASSET by GRAHAM

I can't stand it!

yip yip yap

QUIET!

WOOF

I've got one of my headaches!

HAGAR THE HORRIBLE   By Dik Browne

Questions

(1) Write down the sound-word in *St Pips*. What action is this word representing?

(2) Look at the dog sound-words in *Fred Basset*. Write down all three of them and underline the loudest one.

(3) What action does the sound-word 'thwak!' represent in *Stanley*?

(4) What action does the sound-word 'slurp!' represent in the *Hagar the Horrible* cartoon?

So you can see that with one simple sound-word a cartoonist can seize the attention of the reader. Start collecting cartoon strips with sound-words in them for your class notice-board.

More Sounds and Noises

THE WASHING MACHINE

It goes fwunkety,
    then slunkety,
as the washing goes around.

The water spluncheses,
    and it sluncheses,
as the washing goes around.

As you pick it out it splocheses,
    and it flocheses,
as the washing goes around.

But at the end it schlopperies,
    and then flopperies,
as the washing stops going around.

JEFFREY DAVIES

The Washing Machine — and your own sound-words

(1)   The poet has made up eight sound-words of his own. There are two in each stanza. See whether you can find them and write them down.

(2)   Now try your hand at writing down a word (or two) representing the sounds made by each of the following:
    (a)   someone walking on a sheet of corrugated iron
    (b)   a vacuum-cleaner sucking up the dirt
    (c)   a fisherman throwing out his rod
    (d)   someone trying to start a car which has a flat battery
    (e)   chalk on a blackboard
    (f)   sausages cooking in a pan
    (g)   someone walking through thick mud
    (h)   a fire burning briskly
    (i)   a kettle boiling
    (j)   a cat drinking milk
    (k)   a car running into another car
    (l)   a glass dropping on concrete
    (m)   someone eating potato-chips
    (n)   cats fighting
    (o)   dry leaves being blown along the ground by the wind

(p)　hitting a tennis ball
(q)　a rocket taking off
(r)　a piece of very ripe fruit hitting a wall
(s)　a can of shaken-up soft-drink being opened
(t)　a dentist drilling into your tooth
(u)　a balloon bursting
(v)　a noisy lawnmower
(w)　a typewriter being used by an expert — and then by a non-expert

NOISE

I like noise.
The whoop of a boy, the thud of a hoof,
The rattle of rain on a galvanized roof,
The hubbub of traffic, the roar of a train,
The throb of machinery numbing the brain,
The rush of the wind, a door on the slam,
The switching of wires in an overhead tram,
The boom of the thunder, the crash of the waves,
The din of a river that races and raves,
The crack of a rifle, the clank of a pail,
The strident tattoo of a swift-slapping sail —
Arises a gamut of soul-stirring joys.
I like noise.

JESSIE POPE

Over to you

Now trying writing poems of your own, by filling in the spaces in the three blocks below. The first two spaces in each block have been completed as examples.

I like sounds.
The swish.......... of the ...wind...
The .... of ....
The .... of ....
The .... of ....
The .... of ....
I like sounds.

I like music.
The throb.......... of guitars........
The .... of ....
The .... of ....
The .... of ....
The .... of ....
I like music.

I like sport.
The splash.......... of water
The .... of ....
The .... of ....
The .... of ....
The .... of ....
I like sport.

Now attempt an 'I don't like' poem of your own.

5. Animals and Others

You've all had experiences with dogs. Mostly these experiences are pleasant, but sometimes things go wrong. 'Puppy Problems' is a tale of woe about owning a new dog.

PUPPY PROBLEMS

I bought myself a puppy
And I hoped in time he might
Become my friend and ward off
Things that go bump in the night,
So I put him in a shoe box
And at home I took him out,
And then began to learn
What owning puppies is about.

I tried so hard to love him
And I didn't rave and shout
As he bit into the sofa
And he dragged the stuffing out.
I *gave* him things to chew
But soon I couldn't fail to see
That he liked the things he *found*
More than the things supplied by me.

He frayed my lovely carpet
That I'd saved my pennies for,
And when he wasn't chewing
He was weeing on the floor.
Nor did he spare the table leg
That came in for a gnaw,
Though I told him off the message
Never seemed to reach his jaw.

We laboured at the gardening,
Me and my little pup.
At two I planted flowers
And at four he dug them up.
He liked to dig, he'd bury bones
And pat it down so neat,
And then he'd rush indoors
As clods of mud flew off his feet.

I bought a book on training
And I read it all one night,
And when we set off out
I really thought we'd got it right,
With titbits in my coat
To give him once he got the knack,
But he didn't so I couldn't
So *I* ate them coming back.

When I commanded 'Heel!'
He never seemed to take the point
But galloped on half-strangled,
Tugging my arm out of joint.
He jumped up people's clothes,
The cleaning bills I had to pay!
And when I shouted 'Here!'
He turned and ran the other way.

One day I drove him over
And I gave him to my Dad
Who welcomed him and trained him,
But it left me very sad.
So I thought I'd let you know
In case a pup's in store for you
That it's very wise indeed
To have a Dad who likes dogs too.

                                    PAM AYRES

Puppy Problems — In your opinion

(1) People keep pets for all kinds of reasons. Why did Pam Ayres buy her puppy?

(2) How does the poet show that she had good self-control?

(3) How did the puppy misbehave while he was in the house?

(4) Find evidence to show that the puppy misbehaved in the garden as well.

(5) How did the puppy react to its first owner's training methods?

(6) There are dog-owners who will suggest that Pam Ayres was responsible for some of the bad habits of her puppy. Would you agree? Why?

(7) What would you have done if you had owned her puppy?

(8) Why do you think her Dad was able to train the puppy, while Pam Ayres herself was not?

In your experience

(1) Tell the class about one of the pets you have owned. Describe (a) your pet's appearance and (b) some of the unusual things it did; then (c) explain why you liked it and (d) recall how other people felt about it.

(2) Some people would think that the poet's problems with her puppy are funny. Do you agree?

ADVANTAGE OF FROGS OVER DOGS

I cannot say why Mrs Bray
is so wrapped up with dogs,
when her garden pond and the ditch beyond
are thick on the brim with frogs.

A frog that's green and large and clean,
and disciplined as well,
can be trained to hop to the corner shop
and answer the front-door bell.

When Mrs Bray goes far away
it costs a mint to board her dogs,
but a compost heap, with things that creep,
is all that you need for frogs.

COLIN BINGHAM

Poet's Corner

Dear Girls and Boys,

Please do not think, when you read 'Advantage of Frogs over Dogs', that I would always choose a frog instead of a dog. But the ordinary frog — not the cane toad — has qualities that you and I should recognise.

When I was a small boy in the Queensland outback I lived near a big swamp divided by a road. When the rains came and the swamp was flooded, the frogs at night formed themselves into a huge choir. The tenors and the sopranos were on one side of the road and the baritones and contraltos on the other. No one could guess just where the conductor was, but he was able, in some remarkable way, to stop and start his singers with perfect precision. I used to lie awake listening to them, especially when they sang, 'Hail, hail, O Mighty Storm'.

Years later, when I was a young married man in Brisbane, my wife and I sometimes listened to classical radio programmes in the evening. (There was no TV then.) Nearly always we were joined by a big green frog who came to the open door leading from a verandah. We noticed a special gleam in his eyes when a Beethoven symphony was played.

So you must see why I have written in a kindly way about frogs answering the doorbell and hopping to the corner shop.

Yours pleasantly,
Colin Bingham.

The death of a person or animal we love is usually a difficult emotional experience. This poet does not use a lot of words to tell us how he cared about his dog — we can *feel* the strength of his love. Read the poem through and then discuss the questions that follow.

OLD DOG

Toward the last in the morning she could not
get up, even when I rattled her pan.
I helped her into the yard, but she stumbled
and fell. I knew it was time.

The last night a mist drifted over the fields;
in the morning she would not raise her head —
the far, clear mountains we had walked
surged back to mind.

We looked a slow bargain: our days together
were the ones we already had.
I gave her something the vet had given,
and patted her still, a good last friend.

WILLIAM STAFFORD

Old Dog – Questions for discussion

(1) How *does* the poet convey to us his love for this dog?
(2) What are the *meaning* and the *effect* of 'I knew it was time.'?
(3) How does the poet draw comfort in the last hours of his friend's life?

'Sunning' is another poem about an old dog, yet it is quite different from 'Old Dog'. In 'Sunning' the poet tries to enter the experience of an old dog lying in the sun. The poem's rhythm is relaxed, almost lazy. The rhymes are of an ordinary, 'nothing-fancy' type. The poem is built from a few simple observations — a half-opened winking eye, a scratch, a whimper — and a little poetic imagination.

SUNNING

Old Dog lay in the summer sun
Much too lazy to rise and run.
He flapped an ear
At a buzzing fly.
He winked a half-opened
Sleepy eye.
He scratched himself
On an itching spot,
As he dozed on the porch
Where the sun was hot.
He whimpered a bit
From force of habit
While he lazily dreamed
Of chasing a rabbit.
But Old Dog happily lay in the sun
Much too lazy to rise and run.

JAMES TIPPETT

Try your hand
Write a poem similar in style to 'Sunning'. Choose one of the following subjects.
- a baby lying asleep in its cot
- a tiger lying asleep in its cage
- a shark resting at the bottom of an aquarium
- a kitten asleep against its mother

A CAT

She had a name among the children;
But no one loved though someone owned
Her, locked her out of doors at bedtime
And had her kittens duly drowned.

In Spring, nevertheless, this cat
Ate blackbirds, thrushes, nightingales,
And birds of bright voice and plume and flight,
As well as scraps from neighbours' pails.

I loathed and hated her for this;
One speckle on a thrush's breast
Was worth a million such; and yet
She lived long, till God gave her rest.

EDWARD THOMAS

A Cat – Questions to think about
Different animals inspire different reactions or feelings in people.
(1) How does the poet feel about this cat?
(2) What, in particular, makes him feel this way?
(3) What complaint does he seem to be making in the last couple of lines?

Try your hand
Write a short poem about a creature you dislike. Explain your feelings. Share your results around the class.

from REYNARD THE FOX

The fox was strong, he was full of running,
He could run for an hour and then be cunning,
But the cry behind him made him chill,
They were nearer now and they meant to kill.
They meant to run him until his blood
Clogged on his heart as his brush with mud,
Till his back bent up and his tongue hung flagging,
And his belly and brush were filthed with dragging.
Till he crouched stone-still, dead-beat and dirty,
With nothing but teeth against the thirty.
And all the way to that blinding end
He would meet with men and have none his friend:
Men to holloa and men to run him,
With stones to stagger and yells to stun him;
Men to head him, with whips to beat him,
Teeth to mangle, and mouths to eat him.
And all the way, that wild high crying
To cold his blood with the thought of dying,
The horn and the cheer, and the drum-like thunder
Of the horsehooves stamping the meadows under.
He upped his brush and went with a will
For the Sarsen Stones on Wan Dyke Hill . . .

Seven Sarsens of granite grim,
As he ran them by they looked at him;
As he leaped the lip of their earthen paling
The hounds were gaining and he was failing.

He passed the Sarsens, he left the spur,
He pressed uphill to the blasted fir,
He slipped as he leaped the hedge; he slithered.
'He's mine,' thought Robin. 'He's done; he's dithered.'

At the second attempt he cleared the fence,
He turned half-right where the gorse was dense,
He was leading the hounds by a furlong clear.
He was past his best, but his earth was near.
He ran up gorse to the spring of the ramp,
The steep green wall of the dead men's camp,
He sidled up it and scampered down
To the deep green ditch of the Dead Men's Town.

Within, as he reached that soft green turf,
The wind, blowing lonely, moaned like surf,
Desolate ramparts rose up steep
On either side, for the ghosts to keep.
He raced the trench, past the rabbit warren,
Close-grown with moss which the wind made barren;
He passed the spring where the rushes spread,
And there in the stones was his earth ahead.
One last short burst upon failing feet —
There life lay waiting, so sweet, so sweet,
Rest in a darkness, balm for aches.

The earth was stopped. It was barred with stakes.

JOHN MASEFIELD

Reynard the Fox — Understanding

(1) What are some of the qualities of the fox that might help him to survive?

(2) What are some of the qualities attributed to the men who chase him?

(3) Even the Sarsen Stones appear to have feelings about this fox. How do they seem to view him?

(4) What action of the fox leads Robin to believe that the chase is over?

(5) What is the fox's home called?

(6) How does the fox attempt to throw the hunters off his track? Give one example.

Appreciating

(7) Why does the poet separate the last line?

(8) What feelings towards the fox does the poet seek to arouse in us? How does he do this?

(9) How does the rhythm suit the subject of this poem?

(10) What is the poet's purpose? Do you feel that he is successful in achieving this aim? Give your reasons.

TRAVELLING THROUGH THE DARK

Travelling through the dark I found a deer
dead on the edge of the Wilson River road.
It is usually best to roll them into the canyon:
that road is narrow; to swerve might make more dead.

By glow of the taillight I stumbled back of the car
and stood by the heap, a doe, a recent killing;
she had stiffened already, almost cold.
I dragged her off; she was large in the belly.

My fingers touching her side brought me the reason —
her side was warm; her fawn lay there waiting,
alive, still, never to be born.
Beside that mountain road I hesitated.

The car aimed ahead its lowered parking lights;
under the hood purred the steady engine.
I stood in the glare of the warm exhaust turning red;
around our group I could hear the wilderness listen.

I thought hard for us all — my only swerving —
then pushed her over the edge into the river.

WILLIAM STAFFORD

Travelling through the Dark — A lonely decision

(1) What is the most likely explanation for the presence of the dead deer?
(2) What does the poet mean by 'to swerve might make more dead'?
(3) Explain why the poet hesitates. Why has it suddenly become a big thing to push this deer into the canyon?
(4) 'The car aimed ahead ...' What does the car appear to be wanting to happen?
(5) 'I could hear the wilderness listen.' For what would it be listening?
(6) Why does the poet describe his stopping to think hard as a 'swerving'?
(7) The poem's title describes the man's journey in his car, but to what else might it be referring?
(8) What would you have done if you had been in the poet's position? Give your reasons.

'In Defence of Hedgehogs' is written almost as though a child were talking. It has an innocent, at times quite funny tone. This childlike approach to the subject is clever because it reminds us that children sometimes see simple truths more clearly than do adults.

IN DEFENCE OF HEDGEHOGS

I am very fond of hedgehogs
Which makes me want to say,
That I am struck with wonder,
How there's any left today,
For each morning as I travel
And no short distance that,
All I see are hedgehogs,
Squashed. And dead. And flat.

Now, hedgehogs are not clever,
No, hedgehogs are quite dim,
And when he sees your headlamps,
Well, it don't occur to him,
That the very wisest thing to do
Is up and run away,
No! he curls up in a stupid ball,
And no doubt starts to pray.

Well, motor cars do travel
At a most alarming rate,
And by the time you sees him,
It is very much too late,
And thus he gets a-squasho'd,
Unrecorded but for me,
With me pen and paper,
Sittin' in a tree.

It is statistically proven,
In chapter and in verse,
That in a car and hedgehog fight,
The hedgehog comes off worse,
When whistlin' down your prop shaft,
And bouncin' off your diff,
His coat of nice brown prickles
Is not effect-iff.

A hedgehog cannot make you laugh,
Whistle, dance or sing,
And he ain't much to look at,
And he don't make anything,
And in amongst his prickles,
There's fleas and bugs and that,
But there ain't no need to leave him,
Squashed. And dead. And flat.

Oh spare a thought for hedgehogs,
Spare a thought for me,
Spare a thought for hedgehogs,
As you drink your cup of tea,
Spare a thought for hedgehogs,
Hoverin' on the brinkt,
Spare a thought for hedgehogs,
Lest they become extinct.

PAM AYRES

In Defence of Hedgehogs — Reviewing the poem

(1)   What causes the poet to be 'struck with wonder'?
(2)   What kinds of hedgehogs does she see every morning as she travels?
(3)   What *should* a hedgehog do when it sees headlamps?
(4)   What does it *actually* do?
(5)   What is it about cars that makes them very dangerous for hedgehogs?
(6)   Give the double word that describes what happens when a car meets a hedgehog.
(7)   What do these lines mean?
        'When whistlin' down your prop shaft,
        And bouncin' off your diff,'
(8)   What unpleasant surprise could await you among the hedgehog's prickles?
(9)   The hedgehog, despite its dismal lack of personality, certainly does not deserve its all-too-common fate of being _____ and _____ and _____.
(10)   Why does Pam Ayres want us to spare a thought for the hedgehog?

Discussion Point

Many animal species are threatened with extinction. Why? What could you say about such animals — and the koala is one of them — that would cause people to 'spare a thought'?

The poet Don Marquis wrote a series of poems under the name of 'archy'. Archy is a very intelligent cockroach who satisfies his need to express himself in poetry by jumping up and down on the keyboard of Marquis's unattended typewriter. However, archy finds it impossible to produce capital letters, and, as for punctuation, he ignores that altogether. This explains the absence of both in archy's typing.

Archy refers to Don Marquis — his creator — as 'the boss', and all the boss has to do to find out 'how things look to a cockroach' is to roll a sheet of blank paper into his typewriter and take himself off for a while. Archy does the rest. He emerges from his home inside the typewriter, dances around on the keys and, when his poem is finished, scuttles back inside again. Here are two archy poems for you to read. In the first, 'the lesson of the moth', archy finds out why it is that moths always seem to be trying to burn themselves to death. . . .

THE LESSON OF THE MOTH

i was talking to a moth
the other evening
he was trying to break into
an electric light bulb
and fry himself on the wires

why do you fellows
pull this stunt i asked him
because it is the conventional
thing for moths or why
if that had been an uncovered
candle instead of an electric
light bulb you would
now be a small unsightly cinder
have you no sense

plenty of it he answered
but at times we get tired
of using it
we get bored with the routine
and crave beauty
and excitement
fire is beautiful
and we know that if we get
too close it will kill us

but what does that matter
it is better to be happy
for a moment
and be burned up with beauty
than to live a long time
and be bored all the while

so we wad all our life up
into one little roll
and then we shoot the roll
that is what life is for
it is better to be a part of beauty
for one instant and then cease to
exist than to exist forever
and never be a part of beauty
our attitude toward life
is come easy go easy

we are like human beings
used to be before they became
too civilized to enjoy themselves

and before i could argue him
out of his philosophy
he went and immolated[1] himself
on a patent cigar lighter
i do not agree with him
myself i would rather have
half the happiness and twice
the longevity[2]

but at the same time i wish
there was something i wanted
as badly as he wanted to fry himself

archy
(DON MARQUIS)

1 *immolated*: sacrificed.
2 *longevity*: long life.

The Lesson of the Moth — For you to draw
Draw a comic strip of archy the cockroach talking to the moth. Have them
using some of the words of the poem.

SMALL TALK

i went into the flea circus
on broadway the other day
and heard a lot of fleas
talking and bragging to each other
one flea had been over to the swell dog show
and was boasting that he had bit
a high priced thoroughbred dog
yeah says another flea
that is nothing to get so proud of
a thoroughbred dog tastes just like a mongrel
i should think you would be more democratic
than to brag about that
go and get a reputation
said a third flea
i went into a circus last spring and bit a lion
i completely conquered him
i made him whine and cringe
he did not bite me back
get out of my way
i am the flea that licked a lion
i said to myself probably
that lion didn't even know he had been bitten
some insects are just like human beings
small talk i said to myself
and went away from there

archy the cockroach
(DON MARQUIS)

Notice in these poems how normal punctuation has been disregarded by the poet. Read through 'small talk' and decide with the rest of the class where the normal punctuation marks would fall and what they should be.

Small Talk — Discussion
(1)   What is the effect gained by omitting the punctuation? Why does the poet do this?
(2)   Is this poem really intended to show us something about fleas or cockroaches? What is it really about? Be prepared to argue your point of view.

6. Shaped Poems

Students can derive a lot of enjoyment from writing their own shaped poems. The shape of the poem immediately shows the reader what the poem is about. Have a look at these shaped poems created by students of your own age.

I THINK I'M LOVELY

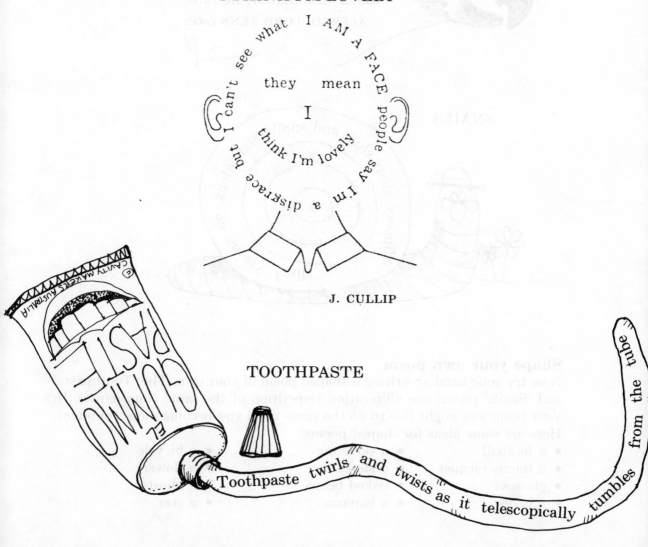

I can't see what they mean I AM A FACE people say I'm a disgrace but I think I'm lovely I

J. CULLIP

TOOTHPASTE

Toothpaste twirls and twists as it telescopically tumbles from the tube

THE EAGLE

He clasps the
crag with crooked
hands; Close to the
sun in lonely lands,
Ringed with the azure world
he stands.
The wrinkled sea
beneath him crawls;
He watches from his
mountain walls, And
like a thunderbolt he falls.

ALFRED, LORD TENNYSON

SNAILS

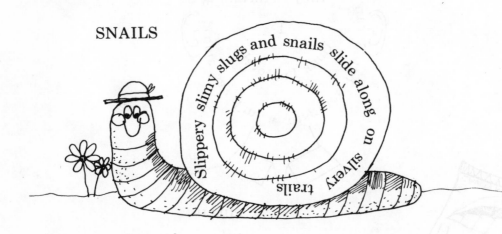

Slippery slimy slugs and snails slide along on silvery trails

Shape your own poem

Now try your hand at writing a shaped poem of your own. The 'Toothpaste' and 'Snails' poems use alliteration (repetition of the same consonants). In your poem you might like to do the same until you become more confident. Here are some ideas for shaped poems:

- a football
- a tennis racquet
- glasses
- scissors
- a skeleton
- a snake
- baked beans
- a banana
- a bicycle
- a flower
- a ghost
- a star

- a cricket bat
- a teapot
- a chair
- an umbrella
- a fish
- a TV set
- an eye, ear or nose
- a face
- a motorcar
- curtains
- a worm
- a fly

You can get many more ideas for shaped poems by holding a class brainstorming session. Each student tries to think up a good subject for a shaped poem. Then the teacher writes the subjects on the board. It's quite amazing how one good idea triggers off another!

Here are some more shaped poems which might give you further ideas.

ACROBATS

IAN HAMILTON FINLAY

THE ANGUISH OF THE MACHINE

```
THE HEAT IS ON TOO MUCH PRESSURE PACKING UP
THE HEAT IS ON TOO MUCH PRESSURE PACKING UP
THE HEAT IS ON TOO MUCH PRESSURE PACKING UP
THE HEAT IS ON TOO MUCH PRESSURE PACKING UP
THE HEAT IS ON TOO MUCH PRESSURE PACKING UP
THE HEAT IS ON TOO MUCH PRESSURE PACKING UP
THE HEAT IS ON TOO MUCH PRESSURE PACKING UP


         CAN'T STAND ANY MORE
         CAN'T STAND ANY MORE
         CAN'T STAND ANY MORE          STRAIN TOO GREAT
         CAN'T STAND ANY MORE          STRAIN TOO GREAT
                                       STRAIN TOO GREAT
DON'T HAVE A BREAK-                    STRAIN TOO GREAT
DOWN DON'T HAVE A                      STRAIN TOO GREAT
BREAK-DOWN DON'T H                     STRAIN TOO GREAT
AVE A BREAK-
DOWN                     DON'T CRACK UP
                              cool down
                              cool down
                              cool down
         don't                cool down
         lose                 cool down
         your                 cool down
         nerv                 cool down
         e                    cool down
         don'
         t
         sto
         pnow

                                  don't

                                            stop now

              don't

              don't
```

PETER MURPHY

FLYING FISH

ALAN RIDDELL

7. The Sea

'Seasonal' means happening only during a certain season of the year. 'Phenomenon' means a remarkable or rare thing or occurrence. After reading through this poem, see whether you can suggest why it is called 'Seasonal Phenomenon'. Keep in mind that the poem has its setting on an American beach, where the swimming season is different from ours.

SEASONAL PHENOMENON

The lifeguard is a man of brawn.
He has a streamlined swim suit on
That fits him like his very skin.
He is not fat, he is not thin;
It is, in fact, his lucky fate
To have no need to watch his weight.
His limbs are trim, his knees unknotted,
His tan is even and unspotted,
He has a profile like Adonis,
And as, with stately, godlike slowness
He regularly paces by,
He wins the soft, admiring eye,
Without half trying to, of each
And every female on the beach.

Oh, let him have his hour of glory —
This creature of a season — for he
Will, as the days grow short, grow sober.
Who cares for lifeguards in October?

RICHARD ARMOUR

Seasonal Phenomenon — Compare the stanzas
(1) What is the poet telling us about the lifeguard in the first stanza?
(2) What happens to the lifeguard in the second stanza?

There is nothing happy or friendly about killing the largest, most harmless living creatures in the world. In fact it is a rather inhuman pursuit, as this poem seeks to show.

KILLING A WHALE

A whale is killed as follows:
A shell is filled with dynamite and
A harpoon takes the shell.
You wait until the great gray back
Breaches the sliding seas, you squint,
Take aim.
The cable snakes like a squirt of paint,
The shell channels deep through fluke
And flank, through mural softness
To bang among the blubber,
Exploding terror through
The hollow fleshy chambers,
While the hooks fly open
Like an umbrella
Gripping the tender tissue.

It dies with some panache,[1]
Whipping the capstan like
A schoolboy's wooden top,
Until the teeth of the machine
Can hold its anger, grip.
Its dead tons thresh for hours
The ravished sea,
Then sink together, sag —
So air is pumped inside
To keep the corpse afloat,
And one of those flags that men
Kill mountains with is stuck
Into this massive death.

Dead whales are rendered down,
Give oil.

                                        DAVID GILL

1 *panache:* display of style; flair

Killing a Whale — Method and message

(1) Re-read the poem and notice the following features that help to make its description and message so real:

    (a) Lines 1–6 read rather like a recipe and this increases the horror of the introduction. Can you say why?

    (b) 'The cable snakes like a squirt of paint' is a vivid simile. See if you can find two other similes in the poem.

    (c) The action of the poem may be divided into five parts. They are:

      lines   1–6   23–28
               7–15   29–30
             16–22

    In your own words, outline what each of these parts contains.

(2) How do you understand the message of this poem? Comment on it.

Pam Ayres now introduces a limpet which offers us some inside information on its lifestyle.

CLAMP THE MIGHTY LIMPET

I am Clamp the Mighty Limpet
I am solid, I am stuck
I am welded to the rockface
With my superhuman suck
I live along the waterline
And in the dreary caves
I am Clamp the Mighty Limpet
I am Ruler of the Waves.

What care I for the shingle,
For the dragging of the tide,
With my unrelenting sucker
And my granite underside?
There's only one reward
For those who come to prise at me
And that's to watch their fingernails
As they go floating out to sea.

Don't upset *me*, I'm a limpet
Though it's plankton I devour
Be very, very careful!
I can move an inch an hour!
Don't you poke or prod me
For I warn you — if you do
You stand there for a fortnight
And I might be stuck on you!

PAM AYRES

Clamp the Mighty Limpet — What does he say?

(1)   What clues tell you that the limpet is very firmly attached to its rock?
(2)   The limpet claims to be the Ruler of the Waves. In what way is this true?
(3)   What is the limpet quite unconcerned about?
(4)   Explain the meaning of 'unrelenting sucker'.
(5)   What happens to those people who prise at the limpet?
(6)   What is the limpet's main food?
(7)   What kind of threat is made in the last stanza?
(8)   Hardly anybody would be worried by this threat. Why?
(9)   What are your feelings about the limpet's lifestyle? Do you feel sorry for it in any way? Why?

THE JELLYFISH

There isn't much a man can do
about a grounded jellyfish
except step over it, or prod
it with his walking stick, and if
he has no walking stick, his shoe.
My feet were bare, so I leaned
to watch the waves relax around
the shiny melted-looking heap.

The jellyfish didn't move,
but then, of course, jellyfishes
don't. They navigate at best
like bottles: When the tide shifts
they bob and drift away. But who
has ever seen a living creature
with a note inside?

I found
an iridescent fish, uneaten
and twitching still, inside the gluey
drying bowel. I saw it jerk,
expand its gills, then quiver, arrested
loosely, loosely and forever.
It shone with pink and green, blue
and yellow, flashed profoundly silver
in each spasm. I knew it was dead
already, and only seemed to work
to free itself.
      As I tried to remove
the notion from my mind, the mound
it moved in, like a glassy brain,
was taken from me by a wave
that slid from the ocean without a sound.

WILLIAM PITT ROOT

The Jellyfish — Some questions

(1) Why does the man in the poem feel helpless when he comes across a grounded jellyfish?
(2) What does he end up doing?
(3) What do jellyfish and bottles have in common?
(4) What does the poet find in the jellyfish that is equivalent, in a strange way, to a note in a bottle?
(5) There are plenty of colours mentioned in the third stanza. See whether you can find the one word in the stanza that stands for all of them.
(6) How does the sea help solve the poet's problem?
(7) A simile in the last stanza compares the jellyfish to a ....
(8) 'The sea is mysterious and looks after its own.' Comment on this statement using ideas and examples from the poem where you can.

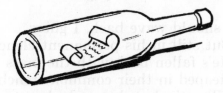

In the poem that follows, two worlds are separated by a pane of glass. In one of them the cold is so terrible that life has almost ceased. In the other there are all the comforting sensations of bustle and life: shouts, the movement of passers-by, and the warmth and leisure of being an interested observer and remembering a past experience.

Yet, a momentary, barely noticeable sign manages to cross from the world of the doomed to the world of the busy living. As you read, ask yourself how you would feel about the ...

LOBSTERS IN THE WINDOW

First, you think they are dead.
Then you are almost sure
One is beginning to stir.
Out of the crushed ice, slow
As the hands of a schoolroom clock,
He lifts his one great claw
And holds it over his head;
Now, he is trying to walk.

But like a run-down toy;
Like the backward crabs we boys
Splashed after in the creek,
Trapped in jars or a net,
And then took home to keep.
Overgrown, retarded, weak,
He is fumbling yet
From the deep chill of his sleep

As if, in a glacial thaw,
Some ancient thing might wake
Sore and cold and stiff
Struggling to raise one claw
Like a defiant fist;
Yet wavering, as if
Starting to swell and ache
With that thick peg in the wrist.

I should wave back, I guess.
But still in his permanent clench
He's fallen back with the mass
Heaped in their common trench
Who stir, but do not look out
Through the rainstreaming glass,
Hear what the newsboys shout,
Or see the raincoats pass.

W. D. SNODGRASS

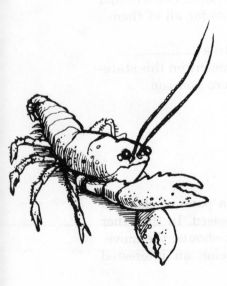

THE SHARK

He seemed to know the harbour,
So leisurely he swam;
His fin,
Like a piece of sheet-iron,
Three-cornered,
And with knife-edge,
Stirred not a bubble
As it moved
With its base-line on the water.

His body was tubular
And tapered
And smoke-blue,
And as he passed the wharf
He turned,
And snapped at a flat-fish
That was dead and floating.
And I saw the flash of a white throat,
And a double row of white teeth,
And eyes of metallic grey,
Hard and narrow and slit.

Then out of the harbour,
With that three-cornered fin,
Shearing without a bubble the water
Lithely,
Leisurely,
He swam —
That strange fish,
Tubular, tapered, smoke-blue,
Part vulture, part wolf,
Part neither — for his blood was cold.

                                    E. J. PRATT

The Shark — Studying the description

(1) What gave the poet the impression that the shark knew the harbour?
(2) 'His fin, Like a piece of sheet-iron . . .' What is this comparison called? Why is the shark's fin like a piece of sheet-iron?
(3) The poet repeats the words 'tubular' and 'tapered'. What pictures do these words give you of the shark?

(4)   The poet repeats 'smoke-blue' and 'white'. What feelings do these colours convey in the context?

(5)   What are the four adjectives used to describe the shark's eyes. What do these words suggest about the shark's temperament?

(6)   Can you suggest why the shark is 'part vulture'?

(7)   Why is the shark 'part wolf'?

(8)   Each of the three stanzas describes a different stage of the shark's progress through the harbour. What are the three stages?

(9)   Briefly list the qualities of the shark described by the poet.

(10) Did you enjoy this poem? Why?

And here's another shark — is he any different? This time a single feature of the shark is stressed: his 'long dark thought'. What *is* the shark's single long dark thought? Why will it never be completed? How about his manners? Try to discover the answers to these questions as you read.

THE SHARK

My sweet, let me tell you about the Shark.
Though his eyes are bright, his thought is dark.
He's quiet — that speaks well of him.
So does the fact that he can swim.
But though he swims without a sound,
Wherever he swims he looks around
With those two bright eyes and that one dark thought.
He has only one but he thinks it a lot.
And the thought he thinks but can never complete
Is his long dark thought of something to eat.
Most anything does. And I have to add
That when he eats, his manners are bad.
He's a gulper, a ripper, a snatcher, a grabber.
Yes, his manners are drab. But his thought is drabber.
That one dark thought he can never complete
Of something — anything — somehow to eat.

Be careful where you swim, my sweet.

JOHN CIARDI

8. Rhyme and Limerick

Rhyme

Probably the simplest rhymes of all are those to be found in 'nursery rhymes', followed closely by those used in limericks. Look at the limerick below. The words in heavy type rhyme with each other, as do the words in italics. Keep in mind that rhyme depends on sound, not on spelling.

There was an old person of **Crewe**
Who found a dead mouse in his **stew.**
Said the waiter : 'Don't *shout*
And wave it *about,*
Or the rest will be wanting one **too!'**

Rhyming pairs

In this list of twenty-four words, there are twelve pairs of rhyming words. Rearrange them in rhyming couples.

tough	toe	enough	bread
dough	here	should	made
stood	plight	mare	pearl
pair	dear	through	die
blue	spite	said	fly
weighed	smile	aisle	twirl

Find rhyming words

Write down words that rhyme with:

spear	past	rusty	sweet	throne	pinch
young	tall	stone	snow	joke	fate
told	taught	house	corn	lace	four
sound	roaring	fruit	white	people	bump
lying	seeing	showers	crow	town	hand

Limericks

Read through the following limericks and notice the rhyming pattern common to them all.

A wonderful bird is the pelican,
His beak can hold more than his belican.
He can take in his beak,
Enough food for a week —
I'm blowed if I know how the helican.

There was a young lady from Niger
Who smiled as she rode on a tiger.
They came back from the ride
With the lady inside
And the smile on the face of the tiger.

There was a young man of Bengal
Who went to a fancy-dress ball.
He went just for fun,
Dressed up as a bun,
And a dog ate him up in the hall.

A tone-deaf old person from Tring,
When somebody asked him to sing,
Replied, 'It is odd
But I cannot tell "God
Save the weasel" from "Pop goes the King".'

There was an old fellow of Lyme
Who married three wives at a time.
When asked: 'Why the third?'
He replied 'One's absurd —
And bigamy, sir, is a crime!'

There was a fat lady of Clyde
Whose shoelaces once came untied.
She feared that to bend
Would display her rear end,
So she cried and she cried and she cried.

There was a young girl of Asturias
Whose temper was frantic and furious.
She used to throw eggs
At her grandmother's legs —
A habit unpleasant, but curious.

The bottle of perfume that Willie sent
Was highly displeasing to Millicent.
Her thanks were so cold
That they quarrelled, I'm told,
Through that silly scent Willie sent Millicent.

There once was a sculptor of mark
Whom they chose to brighten Hyde Park.
Some thought his design
Most markedly fine —
But more liked it best in the dark.

A sea-serpent saw a big tanker,
Bit a hole in her side and then sank her.
It swallowed the crew
In a minute or two,
And then picked its teeth with the anchor.

There was a young lady of Lynn
Who was so excessively thin
That when she essayed
To drink lemonade
She slipped through the straw and fell in.

There was a young lady named Bright
Who travelled much faster than light.
She started one day
In the relative way
And returned on the previous night.

Limerick form

You will have noticed from these limericks that there is a standard, predictable form or pattern that each limerick obeys:

(a)   it has five lines;
(b)   the first, second and fifth lines have one rhyme and the third and fourth lines have a different rhyme;
(c)   the rhythm and number of syllables in lines 1, 2 and 5 match, while the rhythm and number of syllables in lines 3 and 4 also match;
(d)   lines 3 and 4 are short lines.

Because a limerick is never very serious, the last line is usually very important. It is the 'punchline' of the limerick — the line on which the humour of the limerick hinges.

Your turn

(1)   Make a list of as many words as you can that rhyme with the following place-names. Half-rhymes and other 'forced' rhymes may be included (e.g. Sydney — didn't he).

Perth	Kent	Ryde	Parkes	York
St Kilda	Broome	Mars	Calcutta	Hay

(2)   Choose two of the places above and write your own limericks. If you like, use some of the rhyme-words you have already worked out.
(3)   Try to make up limericks of your own using these first lines:
(a)   There was a young lady from Surrey
(b)   A very old man from Tring
(c)   When running along the street to school
(d)   A foolish young man named Joe
(e)   A little old lady from Zee

(4) Write two limericks using some of the following rhyming words. You may choose any three and use them in any order.
   (a) Hobart/slow start/Mozart/go-kart
   (b) Grong Grong/ping-pong/ning-nong/King Kong
   (c) ACT/bee/key/cup of tea/recipe
   (d) Mt Isa/wiser/despise 'er/geyser/miser
   (e) Collingwood/eating pud[ding]/being good

Playing with Words

Many short humorous poems derive their humour from the fact that the poet is 'playing with words'. He may have made up new words; he may have 'forced' some of his rhymes; or he may have simply used a normal word in an unusual way. Read through the following humorous verses, all by anonymous poets.

HOW THE THIEF THOVE

Forth from his den to steal he stole,
His bags full of clink he clunk;
And many a wicked smile he smole,
And many a wink he wunk.

Thump 'n' shake
The plum-sauce bottle;
None'll come
And then a lot'll.

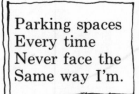

Parking spaces
Every time
Never face the
Same way I'm.

ODE TO A SNEEZE

I sneezed a sneeze into the air,
It fell to earth I know not where;
But hard and froze were the looks of those
In whose vicinity I snooze.

Forth went the thunder-god
Riding on his filly.
'I'm Thor,' he cried.
His horse replied:
'You forgot your thaddle, thilly.'

Your turn

(1) Look at the following lines:

'The little mouse lived with the mice;
He built his house among their hice.'

The rhyme is made by creating a regular, but incorrect, plural. Use this kind of approach to write two rhyming lines of your own on each of the following:

(a) ox/oxen   box/

(b) goose/geese   moose/

(c) brother/brethren   mother/

(d) man/men   can/

(2) Write five short rhyming verses, using each of the five contractions below as one of the rhymes. Note the example:

Packed for holidays.
Off we drive.
Who's forgotten something?
I've!

(a) Can't

(b) We're

(c) We've

(d) They'd

(e) Isn't

9. City Life

For a commuter (a person who travels to and from the city to work) the pace of life is likely to be fast but jerky — happening after happening, and each one different.

The way 'City Life' is written reflects this brisk, jerky pace. Be sensitive to this aspect of the poem as you read through it.

CITY LIFE

City wakes. Sun comes up
Hurried breakfast. Feed the pup
Workers wake. Children dream
Tea or coffee? Milk or cream?

Say Good Morning. Say Good-bye
Quickly leave. Babies cry
Where's the train? Why the fuss?
Never mind, catch a bus

Grab a seat. Down the hill
Women standing. Looks can kill!
Read the paper. Have a smoke
Ignore the cough. Enjoy the joke

Cross the road. Mind the tram
Silly women. Watch that pram!
In the lift. Morning, Jock
Just in time. Beat the clock

Start some work. Have some coffee
File some papers. Chew some toffee
Sign a cheque. Draw a plan
Build a house. Drive a van

Grab a sandwich. That's your lunch
Where's that file? Got a hunch
See the boss. Hope it's short
Might have known. Where's that report?

Grab those plans. Feeling ill
Just my luck. Ink would spill!
Where's my watch? Ten to four
Another letter. Maybe more

Off at last. First one through
Forgot my hat. Join the queue
Grab a taxi. Hurry past
Won't get booked for driving fast.

Have some tea. Take my pills
Read the mail. Only bills
Have a beer. Watch the news
Take a shower. Clean my shoes.

Read a book. Watch a show
Off to bed. Where else to go?
Through the window, starlight peeps
I'm awake. The city sleeps.

Adapted from 'City Life'
JOHN CARDIFF

City Life — Topics and phrases

Look at the table of topics that follows. From the poem, extract one phrase
for each of the topics — a phrase that enlarges on the topic in each case.
The first one has been done to give you the idea.

Topic	Phrase	Topic	Phrase
DAWN	'Sun comes up'	SNACKS	
BREAKFAST		ACCIDENT	
PET		MEDICINE	
BUS		RELAX	
WALKING		TV	
PUNCTUALITY		LIGHTS OUT	

A tournament (old word: *tourney*) was a military sport of the Middle Ages in which knights engaged in combat, mainly on horseback, with spear or sword.

CENTRAL PARK TOURNEY

Cars
In the Park
With long spear lights
Ride at each other
Like armoured knights;
Rush,
Miss the mark,
Pierce the dark,
Dash by!
Another two
Try.

Staged
In the Park
From dusk
To dawn,
The tourney goes on:
Rush,
Miss the mark,
Pierce the dark,
Dash by!
Another two
Try.

MILDRED WESTON

Central Park Tourney — Looking into the poem
(1) What is being compared to Medieval knights at a tournament?
(2) Where is the arena for this modern tournament?
(3) Why is the tourney only from dusk to dawn?
(4) 'With long spear lights . . .' What exactly is meant by this?
(5) Which words in the poem suggest rapid movement?
(6) In both stanzas, the last six lines are the same. What are they describing?
(7) What would it be called, in modern times, if the two combatants did *not* miss the mark?
(8) Why are short, sharp lines appropriate for this poem?

Who but Pam Ayres would write with such feeling, sympathy and gentle humour about a battered mascot wired to the front of a garbage truck?

Notice, as you read through the poem, how certain features of the dolly's appearance — her dress, her rosy cheeks, her squeaker — are shown in their present wretched state and compared with their past state of freshness and charm. In her past life she was happy, until she was replaced ... by what? Why?

As you read, find the lines that amuse you most, and then try to put your finger on the reason for the popularity of Pam Ayres's poetry.

THE DOLLY ON THE DUSTCART

I'm the dolly on the dustcart,
I can see you're not impressed,
I'm fixed above the driver's cab,
With wire across me chest,
The dustman see, he spotted me,
Going in the grinder,
And he fixed me on the lorry,
I dunno if that was kinder.

This used to be a lovely dress,
In pink and pretty shades,
But it's torn now, being on the cart,
And black as the ace of spades,
There's dirt all round me face,
And all across me rosy cheeks,
Well, I've had me head thrown back,
But we ain't had no rain for weeks.

I used to be a 'Mama' doll,
Tipped forward, I'd say 'Mum',
But the rain got in me squeaker,
And now I been struck dumb,
I had two lovely blue eyes,
But out in the wind and weather,
One's sunk back in me head like,
And one's gone altogether.

I'm not a soft, flesh coloured dolly
Modern children like so much,
I'm one of those hard old dollies,
What are very cold to touch,
Modern dolly's underwear
Leaves me a bit nonplussed,
I haven't got a bra,
But then I haven't got a bust!

Yet I was happy in that doll's house,
I was happy as a Queen,
I never knew that Tiny Tears
Was coming on the scene,
I heard of dolls with hair that grew,
And I was quite enthralled,
Until I realised *my* head
Was hard and pink ... and bald.

So I travels with the rubbish,
Out of fashion, out of style,
Out of me environment,
For mile after mile,
No longer prized ... dustbinized!
Unfeminine, Untidy,
I'm the dolly on the dustcart.
There'll be no collection Friday.

PAM AYRES

A madrigal is a type of song, usually about love. As you read the next poem think about the things Mokie hates, and the things he loves. Who, according to Mokie, leads the ideal way of life?

MOKIE'S MADRIGAL

Some little boys get shushed all day,
Can't make noises when they play;
All they do is just annoy —
I want to be a paper-boy;
Paper-boys can ride and ride
Free on all the trams outside,
No-one shushes when they sing,
They can shout like anything:
    Sunnamirra, murdafiar!
    Pyar, pyar! Wannapyar?
    Tirra lirra, tirra lirra!
    Murdafiar, Sunnamirra!

Some little boys can never get
All the ice-creams they could eat;
Paper-boys don't ask their Mums,
They've got bags of treys and brums;
When a paper-boy is full,
He goes and buys a bicycle —
Poppa, Poppa, let me out
To be a paper-boy, and shout:
    Sunnamirra, murdafiar!
    Pyar, pyar! Wannapyar?
    Tirra lirra, tirra lirra!
    Murdafiar, Sunnamirra!

Some little boys can never go
Everywhere they're wanting to;
Paper-boys can choose their track,
Hop on their bikes, and not come back —
Poppa, Poppa, can't you see
How you can get rid of me?
No more Mokie, no more noise,
Only other paper-boys'
    Sunnamirra, murdafiar!
    Pyar, pyar! Wannapyar?
    Tirra lirra, tirra lirra!
    Murdafiar, Sunnamirra!

RONALD MCCUAIG

Mokie's Madrigal — Over to you

(1) What are some of the things that Mokie can't do? In what ways do paper-boys have more freedom than Mokie?

(2) Which lines of the poem most remind you of the lyrics of a song?

(3) From this box of feelings, choose those that apply to Mokie, and explain why.

> envy
> happiness
> discontent
> alarm
> admiration

(4) The words of the 'chorus' are meant to be those actually used by a newsboy as he shouts in his strange paper-seller's language to passers-by. Read the chorus out loud, then write down what you think the words mean in clear English.

(5) What offer does Mokie make to his father at the end of the poem? Do you think his father will think it tempting? Why?

STREET SCENE

A helicopter in the sky
  Observed the traffic down below,
Establishing the where and why
  Of anything that stopped the flow.

A motorist in a crawling queue,
  Distracted by the whirring rotor,
Looked up to get a better view
  And rammed (of course) another motor.

Policemen worked for half the day
  To clear things, and at last succeeded.
The helicopter whirled away
  To see where else it might be needed.

PETER SUFFOLK

Street Scene — Reporting the accident

Now zoom down for a closer look at the scene with this exercise. File a report on the accident outlined in the poem.

ACCIDENT REPORT

TYPE OF ACCIDENT: ....

NO. OF CARS INVOLVED: ....

STATEMENT BY HELICOPTER PILOT ON DUTY: ....
....

STATEMENT BY MOTORIST:
(signed in hospital) ....
....
....

STATEMENT BY POLICE: ....
....
....
....

BLAME FOR ACCIDENT:
(final summing up) ....
....
....

Final thoughts

There is a lesson to be learnt from the events described in 'Street Scene'. What, in your opinion, is this lesson? Does it apply to life in general and not just to this situation? How?

I LIKE THE TOWN

Kids are supposed to like the country—
Because it is natural,
Like them.
And is made up of villages, small
Things, like them.

But I like the town,
With proper white faces
And no empty spaces
Filled with queer noises.

Not the big city,
For that's a pity!
Longwinded like London,
Tottery like Tokyo,
Panting like Paris,
Or choked like Chicago.

But a middling-sized town,
Roads going up,
Streets going down,
And people you know
And people you don't.
In short, just so.

D. J. ENRIGHT

I Like the Town — A question and an activity

(1)   Give the reasons why kids are supposed to like the country.

(2)   Note how four big cities are described in the poem. Supply, from your imagination, an appropriate adjective for each of the following cities.

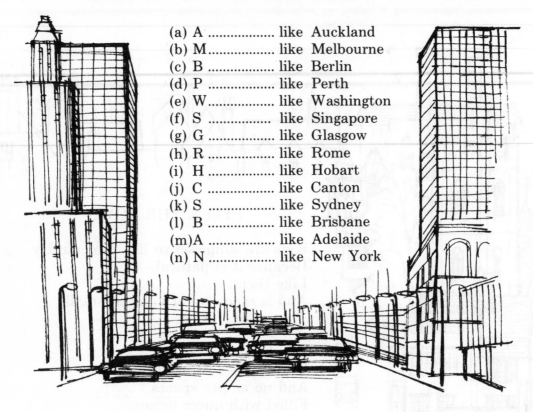

(a) A .... like Auckland
(b) M................. like Melbourne
(c) B .... like Berlin
(d) P .... like Perth
(e) W................. like Washington
(f) S .... like Singapore
(g) G .... like Glasgow
(h) R .... like Rome
(i) H .... like Hobart
(j) C .... like Canton
(k) S .... like Sydney
(l) B .... like Brisbane
(m)A .... like Adelaide
(n) N .... like New York

10. Writing Your First Poems

This unit is designed to give students confidence to start writing poetry of their own. Each section is so structured that all students in the class will have little difficulty in making up poems of their own.

Blackboard Poetry

Read 'Wish Poem' through.

WISH POEM

I wish my father would fall downstairs and break his head;
I wish I had teeth like fingernails;
I wish my fingernails were hard as diamonds;
I wish my sister would explode;
I wish I had a house of my own, my most prized trophy my mother's head;
I wish my other sister would grow thin as a match so I could lose her down a crack;
I wish I had purple ears with yellow spots.

ANONYMOUS

A class 'Wish Poem'

Now the teacher or a student writes up on the board a number of times, 'I wish ...' Then members of the class take turns completing the lines with wishes of their own.

Read the following poem, 'I Saw a Fish-pond All on Fire'.

I SAW A FISH-POND ALL ON FIRE

I saw a fish-pond all on fire,
I saw a house bow to a squire,
I saw a person twelve feet high,
I saw a cottage in the sky,
I saw a balloon made of lead,
I saw a coffin drop down dead,
I saw two sparrows run a race,
I saw two horses making lace,
I saw a girl just like a cat,
I saw a kitten wear a hat,
I saw a man who saw these too,
And said though strange they all were true.

ANONYMOUS

A class 'I Saw . . .' poem

The teacher or a student writes up on the board a number of times, 'I saw . . .' Then members of the class take turns completing the lines with descriptions of their own. This time, as in 'I Saw a Fish-pond All on Fire', each pair of lines must rhyme.

More Poems to Complete

Poems of the senses

Make up poems of your own by completing each of the lines.

I see .... (e.g. a golden sunset)
I hear ....
I feel ....
I smell ....
I taste ....

'Hello/Goodbye' poems

Try some 'Hello/Goodbye' poems. They're very easy.

> Hello holidays, goodbye school.
> Hellow lollies, goodbye teeth.
> Hello ...., goodbye ....
> Hello ...., goodbye ....
> Hello ...., goodbye ....
> Hello ...., goodbye ....
> Hello ...., goodbye ....
> Hello ...., goodbye ....

'Is' poems

Try a few 'Is' poems. The first line of one of the following 'Is' poems has been completed to give you the idea.

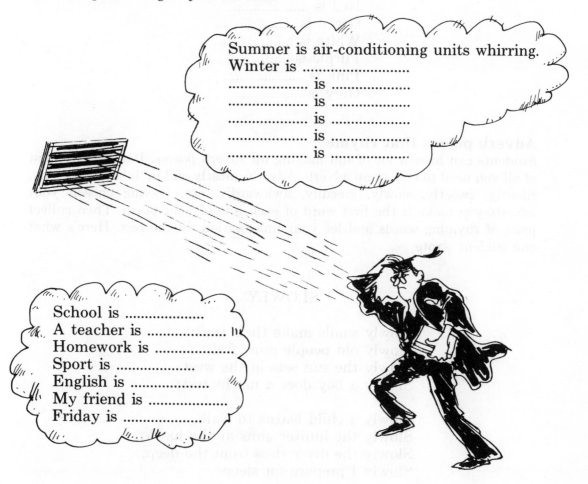

> Summer is air-conditioning units whirring.
> Winter is ....
> .... is ....
> .... is ....
> .... is ....
> .... is ....
> .... is ....

> School is ....
> A teacher is ....
> Homework is ....
> Sport is ....
> English is ....
> My friend is ....
> Friday is ....

'Are' poems

Now, using the same technique, make up some 'Are' poems.

Cats are bundles of fur.
Cars are ....
.... are ....
.... are ....
.... are ....
.... are ....

Colours in poetry

Try your hand at writing a colour poem.

Red is ....
Green is ....
White is ....
Purple is ....
Pink is ....
Grey is ....

Adverb poems that rhyme

Students can have a lot of fun making up adverb poems. It's so easy. First of all you need to choose an adverb. Adverbs mostly end in 'ly' — e.g. angrily, silently, sweetly, slowly, greedily, awkwardly, etc. Having chosen your adverb, you make it the first word of each line of your poem. Then collect pairs of rhyming words and let your imagination do the rest. Here's what one student wrote.

SLOWLY

Slowly snails make their trail;
Slowly old people grow frail;
Slowly the sun sets in the west;
Slowly a boy does a maths test;

Slowly a child learns to walk;
Slowly the hunter aims at the hawk;
Slowly the diver rises from the deep;
Slowly I prepare for sleep.

'Have You Ever Seen a . . .?' poems

Read through these three 'Have you ever seen a ...?' poems, written by students. Then try to write some of your own. Be sure to use plenty of hyphenated words and words ending in '-ed' and '-ing'.

Have you ever seen a tennis player?
Racquet-wielding, sweat-drenched, angry-faced, defeated.

Have you ever seen a fish?
Zig-zagging, shiny-scaled, stream-lined.

Have you ever seen a gorilla?
Pop-eyed, big-mouthed, long-tailed, fat chubby-bellied.

Haiku

A pleasant way of writing your own poetry is to imitate the structure of the Japanese *haiku*. The haiku is a simple but subtle little poem of seventeen syllables. It has three short lines of five, seven, and five syllables respectively. The five haiku that follow have been translated from Japanese into English.

BRAND-NEW KITE

In unending rain
The house-pent boy is fretting
With his brand-new kite.

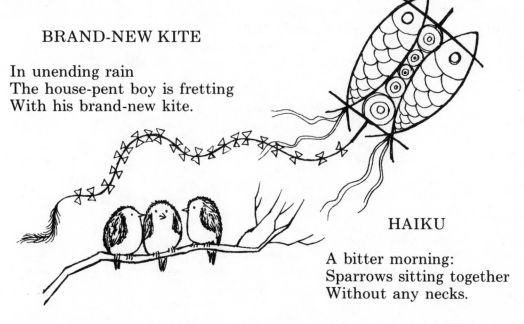

HAIKU

A bitter morning:
Sparrows sitting together
Without any necks.

THE MOON ON THE WATER

Though it be broken —
Broken again — still it's there:
The moon on the water.

AUTUMN

Now the old scarecrow
Looks just like other people ...
Drenching Autumn rain.

FULL MOON

Bright the full moon shines:
On the matting of the floor,
Shadows of the pines.

Copy the pattern of these haiku and create simple picture-poems of
your own. (See if you can express special moods, feelings or ideas, as
in the examples. The 'meaning' of Japanese haiku is often to be found
'beneath the surface' of the description.)

11. A Humorous Look at Ourselves

Australian-born,
Australian-bred,
Long in the legs
And short in the head.

Probably the best-known and best-loved of Australia's humorous poets is the balladist Andrew Barton Paterson. 'Banjo' Paterson (his first poems published in *The Bulletin* were over the pen-name 'The Banjo'!) was born in 1864 near Orange in New South Wales. He went to Sydney Grammar School, and later studied law at university and practised as a lawyer. However, his heart was always in the Australian outback. He loved it, and strove to capture something of its atmosphere — its seriousness and its humour — in his 'fragments of song'.

Paterson's humour is wholesome and enthusiastic, with wide appeal. His outback characters such as Mulga Bill and The Man from Ironbark are vivid and memorable. He has woven these characters into comic situations from which many of Australia's other well-loved, home-grown poems have in turn arisen.

Try getting some of the better readers in the class to read these poems aloud.

Before the mass use of the motorcar and the coming of television, country people tended to behave and dress very differently from city people. Their way of life was much slower and more relaxed. Thus they were looked upon as 'country bumpkins' and a naive country visitor to the city was likely to find himself at the receiving end of a joke. This poem shows us what could happen when the joke got out of hand.

THE MAN FROM IRONBARK

It was the man from Ironbark who struck the Sydney town,
He wandered over street and park, he wandered up and down,
He loitered here, he loitered there, till he was like to drop,
Until at last in sheer despair he sought a barber's shop.
''Ere! shave my beard and whiskers off, I'll be a man of mark,
I'll go and do the Sydney toff up home in Ironbark.'

The barber man was small and flash, as barbers mostly are,
He wore a strike-your-fancy sash, he smoked a huge cigar;
He was a humorist of note and keen at repartee,
He laid the odds and kept a 'tote', whatever that may be,
And when he saw our friend arrive, he whispered 'Here's a lark!
Just watch me catch him all alive, this man from Ironbark.'

There were some gilded youths that sat along the barber's wall,
Their eyes were dull, their heads were flat, they had no brains at all;
To them the barber passed the wink, his dexter eyelid shut,
'I'll make this bloomin' yokel think his bloomin' throat is cut.'
And as he soaped and rubbed it in he made a rude remark:
'I s'pose the flats is pretty green up there in Ironbark.'

A grunt was all reply he got; he shaved the bushman's chin,
Then made the water boiling hot and dipped the razor in.
He raised his hand, his brow grew black, he paused awhile to gloat,
Then slashed the red-hot razor-back across his victim's throat;
Upon the newly-shaven skin it made a livid mark —
No doubt it fairly took him in — the man from Ironbark.

He fetched a wild up-country yell might wake the dead to hear,
And though his throat, he knew full well, was cut from ear to ear,
He struggled gamely to his feet, and faced the murderous foe:
'You've done for me! you dog, I'm beat! one hit before I go!
I only wish I had a knife, you blessed murderous shark!
But you'll remember all your life the man from Ironbark.'

He lifted up his hairy paw, with one tremendous clout
He landed on the barber's jaw, and knocked the barber out.
He set to work with tooth and nail, he made the place a wreck;
He grabbed the nearest gilded youth, and tried to break his neck.
And all the while his throat he held to save his vital spark,
And 'Murder! Bloody Murder!' yelled the man from Ironbark.

A peeler man[1] who heard the din came in to see the show;
He tried to run the bushman in, but he refused to go.
And when at last the barber spoke, and said, ''Twas all in fun —
'Twas just a little harmless joke, a trifle overdone.'
'A joke!' he cried. 'By George, that's fine; a lively sort of lark;
I'd like to catch that murdering swine some night in Ironbark.'

And now while round the shearing floor the listening shearers gape,
He tells the story o'er and o'er, and brags of his escape.
'Them barber chaps what keeps a tote, by George, I've had enough,
One tried to cut my bloomin' throat, but thank the Lord it's tough.'
And whether he's believed or no, there's one thing to remark,
That flowing beards are all the go way up in Ironbark.

A. B. PATERSON

1 *a peeler man:* policeman. Policemen were nicknamed 'Peelers' or 'Bobbies', after Sir
Robert Peel, founder of the first English police force in 1829.

MULGA BILL'S BICYCLE

'Twas Mulga Bill, from Eaglehawk, that caught the cycling craze;
He turned away the good old horse that served him many days;
He dressed himself in cycling clothes, resplendent to be seen;
He hurried off to town and bought a shining new machine;
And as he wheeled it through the door, with air of lordly pride,
The grinning shop assistant said, 'Excuse me, can you ride?'

'See here, young man,' said Mulga Bill, 'from Walgett to the sea,
From Conroy's Gap to Castlereagh, there's none can ride like me.
I'm good all round at everything, as everybody knows,
Although I'm not the one to talk — I hate a man that blows.

'But riding is my special gift, my chiefest, sole delight;
Just ask a wild duck can it swim, a wild cat can it fight.
There's nothing clothed in hair or hide, or built of flesh or steel,
There's nothing walks or jumps, or runs, on axle, hoof or wheel,
But what I'll sit, while hide will hold and girths and straps are
   tight;
I'll ride this here two-wheeled concern right straight away at sight.'

'Twas Mulga Bill, from Eaglehawk, that sought his own abode,
That perched above the Dead Man's Creek, beside the mountain
   road.
He turned the cycle down the hill and mounted for the fray,
But ere he'd gone a dozen yards it bolted clean away.
It left the track, and through the trees, just like a silver streak,
It whistled down the awful slope towards the Dead Man's Creek.

It shaved a stump by half an inch, it dodged a big white-box;
The very wallaroos in fright went scrambling up the rocks,
The wombats hiding in their caves dug deeper underground,
But Mulga Bill, as white as chalk, sat tight to every bound.
It struck a stone and gave a spring that cleared a fallen tree,
It raced beside a precipice as close as close could be;
And then, as Mulga Bill let out one last despairing shriek,
It made a leap of twenty feet into the Dead Man's Creek.

'Twas Mulga Bill, from Eaglehawk, that slowly swam ashore:
He said, 'I've had some narrer shaves and lively rides before;
I've rode a wild bull round a yard to win a five-pound bet,
But this was sure the derndest ride that I've encountered yet.
I'll give that two-wheeled outlaw best; it's shaken all my nerve
To feel it whistle through the air and plunge and buck and swerve.
It's safe at rest in Dead Man's Creek — we'll leave it lying still:
A horse's back is good enough henceforth for Mulga Bill.'

A. B. PATERSON

THE GEEBUNG POLO CLUB

It was somewhere up the country, in a land of rock and scrub,
That they formed an institution called the Geebung Polo Club.
They were long and wiry natives from the rugged mountain side,
And the horse was never saddled that the Geebungs couldn't ride;
But their style of playing polo was irregular and rash —
They had mighty little science, but a mighty lot of dash;
And they played on mountain ponies that were muscular and
    strong.
Though their coats were quite unpolished, and their manes and tails
    were long.
And they used to train those ponies wheeling cattle in the scrub:
They were demons, were the members of the Geebung Polo Club.

It was somewhere down the country in a city's smoke and steam,
That a Polo club existed, called 'The Cuff and Collar Team'.
As a special institution 'twas a marvellous success,
For the members were distinguished by exclusiveness and dress.
They had natty little ponies that were nice, and smooth, and sleek,
For their cultivated owners only rode 'em once a week.
So they started up the country in pursuit of sport and fame,
For they meant to show the Geebungs how they ought to play the
    game;
And they took their valets with them — just to give their boots a
    rub
Ere they started operations on the Geebung Polo Club.

Now my readers can imagine how the contest ebbed and flowed,
When the Geebung boys got going it was time to clear the road;
And the game was so terrific that ere half the time was gone
A spectator's leg was broken — just from merely looking on.
For they waddied one another till the plain was strewn with dead,
While the score was kept so even that they neither got ahead.
And the Cuff and Collar Captain, when he tumbled off to die
Was the last surviving player — so the game was called a tie.

Then the Captain of the Geebungs raised him slowly from the
  ground,
Though his wounds were mostly mortal, yet he fiercely gazed
  around;
There was no one to oppose him — all the rest were in a trance,
So he scrambled on his pony for his last expiring chance,
For he meant to make an effort to get victory to his side;
So he struck at goal — and missed it — then he tumbled off and
  died.

By the old Campaspe River, where the breezes shake the grass,
There's a row of little gravestones that the stockmen never pass,
For they bear a rude inscription saying, 'Stranger, drop a tear,
For the Cuff and Collar players and the Geebung boys lie here.'

And on misty moonlit evenings, while the dingoes howl around,
You can see their shadows flitting down that phantom polo ground;
You can hear the loud collisions as the flying players meet,
And the rattle of the mallets, and the rush of ponies' feet,
Till the terrified spectator rides like blazes to the pub —
He's been haunted by the spectres of the Geebung Polo Club.

                                                    A. B. PATERSON

The Geebung Polo Club — Looking more closely

(1) Would you class this poem as humorous or sad? Why?
(2) What kind of people were the members of the Geebung Polo Club?
(3) What were their ponies like?
(4) How were the members of The Cuff and Collar Team different from
     those of the Geebung Polo Club?
(5) What do you know about the ponies that The Cuff and Collar Team
     possessed?
(6) What is the meaning of 'his wounds were mostly mortal'?
(7) What comments would you make about the character of the Captain
     of the Geebungs?
(8) Do you think that the poet has exaggerated some of the happenings
     in this poem? Why?
(9) Which team did you prefer? Give your reasons?
(10) Did you enjoy the poem? Why or why not?

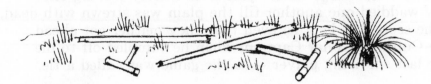

The next poem by 'Banjo' Paterson doesn't feature 'heroic' outback characters. It is simply woven around a comic incident.

A BUSH CHRISTENING

On the outer Barcoo where the churches are few,
    And men of religion are scanty,
On a road never cross'd 'cept by folk that are lost
    One Michael Magee had a shanty.

Now this Mike was the dad of a ten-year-old lad,
    Plump, healthy, and stoutly conditioned;
He was strong as the best, but poor Mike had no rest
    For the youngster had never been christened.

And his wife used to cry, 'If the darlin' should die,
    Saint Peter would not recognize him.'
But by luck he survived till a preacher arrived,
    Who agreed straightaway to baptize him.

Now the artful young rogue, while they held their collogue,
    With his ear to the keyhole was listenin';
And he muttered in fright, while his features turned white,
    'What the divil and all is this christenin'?'

He was none of your dolts — he had seen them brand colts,
    And it seemed to his small understanding;
If the man in the frock made him one of the flock,
    It must mean something very like branding.

So away with a rush he set off for the bush,
    While the tears in his eyelids they glistened —
''Tis outrageous,' says he, 'to brand youngsters like me;
    I'll be dashed if I'll stop to be christened!'

Like a young native dog he ran into a log,
    And his father with language uncivil,
Never heeding the 'praste', cried aloud in his haste,
    'Come out and be christened, you divil!'

But he lay there as snug as a bug in a rug,
    And his parents in vain might reprove him,
Till his reverence spoke (he was fond of a joke),
    'I've a notion,' says he, 'that'll move him.

'Poke a stick up the log, give the spalpeen a prod;
  Poke him aisy — don't hurt him or maim him;
'Tis not long that he'll stand, I've the water at hand,
  As he rushes out this end I'll name him.

'Here he comes, and for shame! ye've forgotten the name —
  Is it Patsy or Michael or Dinnis?'
Here the youngster ran out, and the priest gave a shout —
  'Take your chance, anyhow, wid 'Maginnis!''

As the howling young cub ran away to the scrub
  Where he knew that pursuit would be risky,
The priest, as he fled, flung a flask at his head
  That was labelled 'Maginnis's Whisky'!

Now Maginnis Magee has been made a JP,
  And the one thing he hates more than sin is
To be asked by the folk, who have heard of the joke,
  How he came to be christened Maginnis!

                                        A. B. PATERSON

A Bush Christening — Points to consider
(1) Why would this poem be classed as a *humorous* ballad?
(2) Pick out three words from the poem that are written with an 'Irish' pronunciation.
(3) Explain why the young boy became so frightened.
(4) 'And his father with language uncivil . . .' How was Michael actually talking?
(5) Where, according to Paterson, did this incident take place?
(6) Why did the priest think of the name 'Maginnis'?
(7) Explain why the priest had the flask in his hand.
(8) What is a JP? Why would this story have been upsetting to a man who had been made a JP?

Here is another of 'Banjo' Paterson's poems, this one having its setting at Walgett. Walgett is a town on the Darling River and for many years it was considered one of the last outposts of civilisation in the far north-west of New South Wales.

BEEN THERE BEFORE

There came a stranger to Walgett town,
To Walgett town when the sun was low,
And he carried a thirst that was worth a crown,
Yet how to quench it he did not know;
But he thought he might take those yokels down,
The guileless yokels of Walgett town.

They made him a bet in a private bar,
In a private bar when the talk was high,
And they bet him some pounds no matter how far
He could pelt a stone, yet he could not shy
A stone right over the river so brown,
The Darling River at Walgett town.

He knew that the river from bank to bank
Was fifty yards, and he smiled a smile
As he trundled down; but his hopes they sank,
For there wasn't a stone within fifty mile;
For the saltbush plain and the open down
Produce no quarries in Walgett town.

The yokels laughed at his hopes o'erthrown,
And he stood awhile like a man in a dream;
Then out of his pocket he fetched a stone,
And pelted it over the silent stream —
He'd been there before; he had wandered down
On a previous visit to Walgett town.

A. B. PATERSON

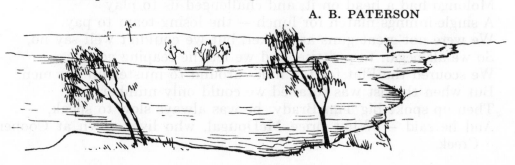

Analysing the humour in Paterson's poems

(1) What are some of the qualities Paterson seems to see in bush people in his poems?

(2) What are some of the qualities Paterson seems to see in city people in his poems?

(3) In what way (if any) are the bush people made to seem superior to the city people in these poems?

(4) Which poem has most appeal for you? Give reasons for your choice.

(5) Which are more important, the *characters* or the *situations*, to the effectiveness of the humour in Paterson's poems?

Thomas Spencer emigrated to Australia as a young man in 1863. He returned to England for some years before finally settling in Australia in 1875, where he became a successful building contractor. His description of a country cricket match has become one of the humorous classics of Australian verse.

HOW McDOUGAL TOPPED THE SCORE

A peaceful spot is Piper's Flat. The folk that live around —
They keep themselves by keeping sheep and turning up the ground;
But the climate is erratic, and the consequences are
The struggle with the elements is everlasting war.
We plough, and sow, and harrow — then sit down and pray for rain;
And then we all get flooded out and have to start again.
But the folk are now rejoicing as they ne'er rejoiced before,
For we've played Molongo cricket, and McDougal topped the score!

Molongo had a head on it, and challenged us to play
A single-innings match for lunch — the losing team to pay.
We were not great guns at cricket, but we couldn't well say no,
So we all began to practise, and we let the reaping go.
We scoured the Flat for ten miles around to muster up our men,
But when the list was totalled we could only number ten.
Then up spoke big Tim Brady: he was always slow to speak,
And he said — 'What price McDougal, who lives down at Cooper's
    Creek.'

So we sent for old McDougal, and he stated in reply
That he'd never played at cricket, but he'd half a mind to try.
He couldn't come to practise — he was getting in his hay,
But he guessed he'd show the beggars from Molongo how to play.
Now, McDougal was a Scotchman, and a canny one at that,
So he started in to practise with a paling for a bat.
He got Mrs Mac to bowl to him, but she couldn't run at all,
So he trained his sheep-dog, Pincher, how to scout and fetch the
    ball.

Now, Pincher was no puppy; he was old, and worn, and grey;
But he understood McDougal, and — accustomed to obey —
When McDougal cried out 'Fetch it!' he would fetch it in a trice,
But, until the word was 'Drop it!' he would grip it like a vice.
And each succeeding night they played until the light grew dim;
Sometimes McDougal struck the ball — sometimes the ball struck
    him.
Each time he struck, the ball would plough a furrow in the ground;
And when he missed, the impetus would turn him three times
    round.

The fatal day at length arrived — the day that was to see
Molongo bite the dust, or Piper's Flat knocked up a tree!
Molongo's captain won the toss, and sent his men to bat,
And they gave some leather-hunting to the men of Piper's Flat.
When the ball sped where McDougal stood, firm planted in his
    track,
He shut his eyes, and turned him round, and stopped it — with his
    back!
The highest score was twenty-two, the total sixty-six,
When Brady sent a yorker down that scattered Johnson's sticks.

Then Piper's Flat went in to bat, for glory and renown,
But, like the grass before the scythe, our wickets tumbled down.
'Nine wickets down for seventeen, with fifty more to win!'
Our captain heaved a heavy sigh, and sent McDougal in.
'Ten pounds to one you'll lose it!' cried a barracker from town;
But McDougal said, 'I'll tak' it, mon!' and planked the money down.
Then he girded up his moleskins in a self-reliant style,
Threw off his hat and boots and faced the bowler with a smile.

He held the bat the wrong side out, and Johnson with a grin
Stepped lightly to the bowling crease, and sent a 'wobbler' in;
McDougal spooned it softly back, and Johnson waited there,
But McDougal, crying 'Fetch it!' started running like a hare.
Molongo shouted 'Victory! He's out as sure as eggs,'
When Pincher started through the crowd, and ran through Johnson's
    legs.
He seized the ball like lightning; then he ran behind a log,
And McDougal kept on running, while Molongo chased the dog!

They chased him up, they chased him down, they chased him round
    and then
He darted through the slip-rail as the scorer shouted 'Ten!'
McDougal puffed; Molongo swore; excitement was intense;
As the scorer marked down twenty, Pincher cleared a barbed-wire
    fence.
'Let us head him!' shrieked Molongo. 'Brain the mongrel with a
    bat!'
'Run it out! Good old McDougal!' yelled the men of Piper's Flat.
And McDougal kept on jogging, and then Pincher doubled back,
And the scorer counted 'Forty' as they raced across the track.

McDougal's legs were going fast, Molongo's breath was gone —
But still Molongo chased the dog — McDougal struggled on.
When the scorer shouted 'Fifty' then they knew the chase could
    cease,
And McDougal gasped out 'Drop it!' as he dropped within his
    crease.
Then Pincher dropped the ball, and as instinctively he knew
Discretion was the wiser plan, he disappeared from view;
And as Molongo's beaten men exhausted lay around
We raised McDougal shoulder-high, and bore him from the ground.

We bore him to McGiniss's, where lunch was ready laid,
And filled him up with whisky-punch, for which Molongo paid.
We drank his health in bumpers and we cheered him three times
    three,
And when Molongo got its breath Molongo joined the spree
And the critics say they never saw a cricket match like that,
When McDougal broke the record in the game at Piper's Flat;
And the folk are jubilating as they never did before;
For we played Molongo cricket — and McDougal topped the score!

THOMAS E. SPENCER

How McDougal Topped the Score — A closer look

(1)   Many of the phrases used in this poem are 'bush' expressions — colourful phrases that have since become common slang expressions. In the table below, match some of these colourful phrases from the poem with their correct meanings.

Phrases from poem	Meanings
not great guns	thoroughly defeated
he'd half a mind	definitely
bite the dust	scored a lot of runs
knocked up a tree	not very good
gave some leather-hunting	he was inclined
as sure as eggs	soundly thrashed

(2)   What is a 'canny' Scotchman? Explain how McDougal was canny.

(3)   What made Johnson grin as he came in to bowl at McDougal?

(4)   What did Pincher do that was discreet after dropping the ball? Why was this action a discreet one?

Appreciating

(5)   What sort of a 'picture' does this poem give us of Piper's Flat and its people?

(6)   What is the effect of the short word-groups in the line, 'McDougal puffed; Molongo swore; excitement was intense;'?

It was to be expected that humorous poems by an Irish Roman Catholic priest might include some mention of the Church, and some description of the funnier sides of bush people and bush life. Father P. J. Hartigan, serving the Church at Goulburn and Narrandera, was such a man, and among his poems are such humorous gems as 'Said Hanrahan' and 'Tangmalangaloo'. He wrote much of his poetry under the pen-name, 'John O'Brien'.

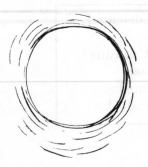

SAID HANRAHAN

'We'll all be rooned,' said Hanrahan,
    In accents most forlorn,
Outside the church, ere Mass began,
    One frosty Sunday morn.

The congregation stood about,
    Coat-collars to the ears,
And talked of stock, and crops, and drought,
    As it had done for years.

'It's lookin' crook,' said Daniel Croke;
    'Bedad, it's cruke, me lad,
For never since the banks went broke
    Has seasons been so bad.'

'It's dry, all right,' said young O'Neil,
    With which astute remark
He squatted down upon his heel
    And chewed a piece of bark.

And so around the chorus ran
    'It's keeping dry, no doubt.'
'We'll all be rooned,' said Hanrahan,
    'Before the year is out.

'The crops are done; ye'll have your work
    To save one bag of grain;
From here way out to Back-o'-Bourke
    They're singin' out for rain.'

'They're singing' out for rain,' he said,
  'And all the tanks are dry.'
The congregation scratched its head,
  And gazed around the sky.

'There won't be grass, in any case,
  Enough to feed an ass;
There's not a blade on Casey's place
  As I came down to Mass.'

'If rain don't come this month,' said Dan,
  And cleared his throat to speak —
'We'll all be rooned,' said Hanrahan,
  'If rain don't come this week.'

A heavy silence seemed to steal
  On all at this remark;
And each man squatted on his heel,
  And chewed a piece of bark.

'We want an inch of rain, we do,'
  O'Neil observed at last;
But Croke 'maintained' we wanted two
  To put the danger past.

'If we don't get three inches, man,
  Or four to break this drought,
We'll all be rooned,' said Hanrahan,
  'Before the year is out.'

In God's good time down came the rain;
  And all the afternoon
On iron roof and window-pane
  It drummed a homely tune.

And through the night it pattered still,
  And lightsome, gladsome elves
On dripping spout and window-sill
  Kept talking to themselves.

It pelted, pelted all day long,
  A-singing at its work,
Till every heart took up the song
  Way out to Back-o'-Bourke.

And every creek a banker ran,
 And dams filled overtop;
'We'll all be rooned,' said Hanrahan,
 'If this rain doesn't stop.'

And stop it did, in God's good time;
 And spring came in to fold
A mantle o'er the hills sublime
 Of green and pink and gold.

And days went by on dancing feet,
 With harvest-hopes immense,
And laughing eyes beheld the wheat
 Nid-nodding o'er the fence.

And, oh, the smiles on every face,
 As happy lad and lass
Through grass knee-deep on Casey's place
 Went riding down to Mass.

While round the church in clothes genteel
 Discoursed the men of mark,
And each man squatted on his heel,
 And chewed his piece of bark.

'There'll be bush-fires for sure, me man,
 There will, without a doubt;
We'll all be rooned,' said Hanrahan,
 'Before the year is out.'

JOHN O'BRIEN

Said Hanrahan — Class discussion

Hanrahan might be described as the eternal pessimist (a person who always expects the worst). No matter what occurs, he will always perceive some danger, some problem, associated with it. In your class, discuss whether or not being pessimistic is 'typically Australian'. Are most Australians pessimistic? Do we have a 'national character'? If so, what are some of the qualities you see as part of our national character?

W. T. Goodge was another humorous poet who wrote for *The Bulletin* in the 1890s. This poem depends for its humour upon the unexpected (or is it?) ending.

A SNAKE YARN

'You talk of snakes,' said Jack the Rat,
    'But blow me, one hot summer,
I seen a thing that knocked me flat —
Fourteen foot long or more than that,
    It was a reg'lar hummer!
Lay right along a sort of bog,
               Just like a log!

'The ugly thing was lyin' there
    And not a sign o' movin',
Give any man a nasty scare;
Seen nothin' like it anywhere
    Since I first started drovin'.
And yet it didn't scare my dog.
              Looked like a log!

'I had to cross that bog, yer see,
    And bluey I was humpin';
But wonderin' what that thing could be
A-lyin' there in front o' me
    I didn't feel like jumpin'.
Yet, though I shivered like a frog,
            It *seemed* a log!

'I takes a leap and lands right on
    The back of that there whopper!'
He stopped. We waited. Then Big Mac
Remarked: 'Well, then, what happened, Jack?'
'Not much,' said Jack, and drained his grog.
            'It *was* a log!'

                            W. T. GOODGE

Edward Harrington, a Victorian, served as a cavalryman in World War I before returning to Australia to try his hand at farming. To complete this brief look at some of the best of Australian humorous poems, read through the one by Harrington that follows.

'THERE'S ONLY TWO OF US HERE'

I camped one night in an empty hut on the side of a lonely hill;
I didn't go much on empty huts, but the night was awful chill.
So I boiled me billy and had me tea, and seen that the door was
    shut,
Then I went to bed in an empty bunk by the side of the old slab
    hut.

It must have been about twelve o'clock — I was feeling cosy and
    warm —
When at the foot of me bunk I see a horrible ghostly form.
It seemed in shape to be half an ape with a head like a chimpanzee,
But wot the 'ell was it doin' there, and wot did it want with me?

You may say if you please that I had d.ts or call me a crimson liar,
But I wish you had seen it as plain as me with its eyes like coals
    of fire!
Then it gave a moan and a horrible groan that curdled me blood with
    fear,
And, 'There's only two of us here,' it ses; 'there's only two of us
    here!'

I kept one eye on the old hut door and one on the awful brute;
I only wanted to dress meself and get to the door and scoot.
But I couldn't find where I'd left me boots so I hadn't a chance to
    clear;
And, 'There's only two of us here,' it moans, 'there's only two of us
    here!'

I hadn't a thing to defend meself, not even a stick or stone;
And, 'There's only two of us here!' it ses again with a horrible
    groan.
I thought I'd better make some reply, though I reckoned me end was
    near:
'By the holy smoke, when I finds me boots there'll be only one of
    us here!'

I gets me hands on me number tens and out through the door I
   scoots,
And I lit the whole of the hillside up with the sparks from me blucher
   boots.
So I've never slept in a hut since then, and I tremble and shake with
   fear
When I think of that horrible form wot moaned, 'There's only two
   of us here!'

EDWARD HARRINGTON

'There's Only Two of Us Here' — Understanding

(1)   What are d.ts?
(2)   What are the poet's 'number tens'?
(3)   'And I lit the whole of the hillside up with the sparks from me blucher
      boots.' What does this line picture the swaggie doing?
(4)   In spite of his fear, the swaggie seems to keep his sense of humour.
      Where is this shown in the poem?

Appreciating

(5)   Pick out some examples of mis-spelling in the poem. How does such
      spelling help to create a picture of this swagman? What sort of picture
      does it create?
(6)   Pick out some examples of special use of language that adds to the
      picture of the swaggie. How well does it fit his character?
(7)   Would this poem be better without the last verse? Give a reason for
      your answer.

Verse-speaking

As with many Australian humorous ballads, this is an excellent one to learn
by heart as a class. The effort involved in learning will be more than repaid
by the pleasure of being able to recite the poem for other classes. Why not
work at it?

12. Rhythm

Rhythm is the swing or the beat that can run so effectively through lines of poetry. Read through John Masefield's poem, 'Cargoes'.

CARGOES

Quinquireme of Nineveh from distant Ophir,
Rowing home to haven in sunny Palestine,
With a cargo of ivory,
And apes and peacocks,
Sandalwood, cedarwood, and sweet white wine.

Stately Spanish galleon coming from the Isthmus,
Dipping through the Tropics by the palm-green shores,
With a cargo of diamonds,
Emeralds, amethysts,
Topazes, and cinnamon, and gold moidores.

Dirty British coaster with a salt-caked smoke stack,
Butting through the Channel in the mad March days,
With a cargo of Tyne coal,
Road-rails, pig-lead,
Firewood, iron-ware, and cheap tin trays.

JOHN MASEFIELD

Cargoes — For you to think about
(1) A quinquireme was, in Roman times, a ship with five banks of oars. With this clue in mind, what is the rhythm of the first stanza of the poem?
(2) To what is the rhythm of the second stanza similar?
(3) What is being described in the third stanza? Is the rhythm faster than in the other two stanzas? Why? What does the beat or rhythm resemble?

Here is a poem about a fence.

THE PICKETY FENCE

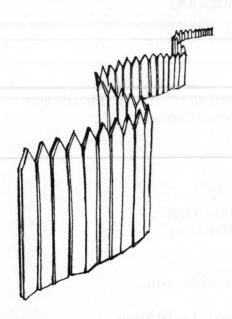

The pickety fence,
The pickety fence,
Give it a lick it's
The pickety fence
Give it a lick it's
The clickety fence
Give it a lick it's
A lickety fence
Give it a lick
Give it a lick
Give it a lick
With a rickety stick
Pickety
Pickety
Pickety
Pick.

DAVID McCORD

The Pickety Fence — What did you hear?
It seems strange to think that a fence can have rhythm, but if you read the poem to yourself you'll be quite aware of it. Can you identify the rhythm? What is it?

Identifying the rhythm or movement
Look at the lines of poetry below. Read them to yourself, savour the rhythms, then try to identify the particular rhythm or movement used in each.

(1)   This is the night mail crossing the border,
      Bringing the cheque and the postal order,
      Letters for the rich, letters for the poor,
      The shop at the corner and the girl next door.

(2)   Click go the shears boys, click, click, click;
      Wide is his blow and his hands move quick;
      The ringer looks round and is beaten by a blow,
      And curses the old snagger with the bare-bellied yeo.

(3)   Half a league, half a league,
Half a league onward,
All in the valley of Death
Rode the six hundred.

Here is a famous love-story full of romance, adventure — and tragedy.

THE HIGHWAYMAN

Part One

The wind was a torrent of darkness among the gusty trees,
The moon was a ghostly galleon tossed upon cloudy seas,
The road was a ribbon of moonlight over the purple moor,
And the highwayman came riding —
   Riding — riding —
The highwayman came riding, up to the old inn-door.

He'd a French cocked-hat on his forehead, a bunch of lace at his
    chin,
A coat of the claret velvet, and breeches of brown doe-skin;
They fitted with never a wrinkle: his boots were up to the thigh!
And he rode with a jewelled twinkle,
   His pistol butts a-twinkle,
His rapier hilt a-twinkle, under the jewelled sky.

Over the cobbles he clattered and clashed in the dark inn-yard,
And he tapped with his whip on the shutters, but all was locked and
    barred;
He whistled a tune to the window, and who should be waiting there
But the landlord's black-eyed daughter,
   Bess, the landlord's daughter,
Plaiting a dark red love-knot into her long black hair.

And dark in the dark old inn-yard a stable-wicket creaked
Where Tim the ostler listened; his face was white and peaked;
His eyes were hollows of madness, his hair like mouldy hay,
But he loved the landlord's daughter,
   The landlord's red-lipped daughter.
Dumb as a dog he listened, and he heard the robber say —

'One kiss, my bonny sweetheart, I'm after a prize to-night,
But I shall be back with the yellow gold before the morning light;
Yet, if they press me sharply, and harry me through the day,
Then look for me by moonlight,
  Watch for me by moonlight,
I'll come to thee by moonlight, though hell should bar the way.'

He rose upright in the stirrups; he scarce could reach her hand,
But she loosened her hair i' the casement! His face burned like a
  brand
As the black cascade of perfume came tumbling over his breast;
And he kissed its waves in the moonlight,
  (Oh, sweet black waves in the moonlight!)
Then he tugged at his rein in the moonlight, and galloped away to
  the West.

Part Two

He did not come in the dawning; he did not come at noon;
And out o' the tawny sunset, before the rise o' the moon,
When the road was a gipsy's ribbon, looping the purple moor,
A red-coat troop came marching —
  Marching — Marching —
King George's men came marching, up to the old inn-door.

They said no word to the landlord, they drank his ale instead,
But they gagged his daughter and bound her to the foot of her narrow
  bed;
Two of them knelt at her casement, with muskets at their side!
There was death at every window;
  And hell at one dark window;
For Bess could see, through her casement, the road that *he* would
  ride.

They had tied her up to attention, with many a sniggering jest;
They had bound a musket beside her, with the muzzle beneath her
  breast!
'Now keep good watch!' and they kissed her.
She heard the dead man say —
Look for me by moonlight;
  Watch for me by moonlight;
I'll come to thee by moonlight, though hell should bar the way!'

She twisted her hands behind her; but all the knots held good!
She writhed her hands till her fingers were wet with sweat or blood!
They stretched and strained in the darkness, and the hours crawled
    by like years,
Till, now, on the stroke of midnight,
  Cold, on the stroke of midnight,
The tip of one finger touched it! The trigger at least was hers!

The tip of one finger touched it; she strove no more for the rest!
Up, she stood up to attention, with the muzzle beneath her breast,
She would not risk their hearing; she would not strive again;
For the road lay bare in the moonlight;
  Blank and bare in the moonlight;
And the blood of her veins in the moonlight throbbed to her love's
    refrain.

Tlot-tlot, tlot-tlot! Had they heard it? The horse-hoofs ringing clear;
Tlot-tlot, tlot-tlot, in the distance? Were they deaf that they did not
    hear?
Down the ribbon of moonlight, over the brow of the hill,
The highwayman came riding,
  Riding, riding!
The red-coats looked to their priming! She stood up straight and
    still!

Tlot-tlot, in the frosty silence! *Tlot-tlot,* in the echoing night!
Nearer he came and nearer! Her face was like a light!
Her eyes grew wide for a moment; she drew one last deep breath,
Then her finger moved in the moonlight,
  Her musket shattered the moonlight,
Shattered her breast in the moonlight and warned him — with her
    death.

He turned; he spurred to the Westward; he did not know who stood
Bowed, with her head o'er the musket, drenched with her own red
    blood!
Not till the dawn he heard it, and his face grew grey to hear
How Bess, the landlord's daughter,
  The landlord's black-eyed daughter,
Had watched for her love in the moonlight, and died in the darkness
    there.

Back, he spurred like a madman, shrieking a curse to the sky,
With the white road smoking behind him and his rapier brandished
    high!
Blood-red were his spurs i' the golden noon; wine-red was his velvet
    coat;
When they shot him down on the highway,
   Down like a dog on the highway,
And he lay in his blood on the highway, with the bunch of lace at
    his throat.

       .   .   .   .

And still of a winter's night, they say, when the wind is in the trees,
When the moon is a ghostly galleon tossed upon cloudy seas,
When the road is a ribbon of moonlight over the purple moor,
A highwayman comes riding —
   Riding — riding —
A highwayman comes riding, up to the old inn-door.

Over the cobbles he clatters and clangs in the dark inn-yard;
And he taps with his whip on the shutters, but all is locked and
    barred;
He whistles a tune to the window, and who should be waiting there
But the landlord's black-eyed daughter,
   Bess, the landlord's daughter,
Plaiting a dark red love-knot into her long black hair.

ALFRED NOYES

The Highwayman — Closer scrutiny
(1)   What words convey the movement of the wind?
(2)   What words suggest the rhythm of the highwayman on horseback as
       he approaches the inn?
(3)   'The moon was a ghostly galleon' and 'The road was a ribbon of moon-
       light' are both metaphors. What picture do these metaphors bring to
       your mind?
(4)   In the poem we are told how the highwayman was dressed. What do
       you learn about his character from this description?
(5)   'Over the cobbles he clattered and clashed ...' What words here
       suggest the actual sounds that the highwayman and his horse were
       making?

(6)   'His hair like mouldy hay' and 'Dumb as a dog he listened' are both examples of what figure of speech?

(7)   What firm promise did the highwayman make to Bess?

(8)   Who betrayed the highwayman to the soldiers? Why? Give evidence from the poem.

(9)   'There was death at every window' and 'hell at one dark window'. Why was there hell at one window in particular?

(10) 'She heard the dead man say ...' Why 'the dead man'?

(11) By midnight, what had Bess managed to do?

(12) How did Bess warn her highwayman?

(13) How did the highwayman react?

(14) When he heard, at dawn, the news of Bess's sacrifice, what change came over him?

(15) 'Back, he spurred ... brandished high!' There's a fast and furious rhythm in these lines. Can you explain why?

(16) The last word on the highwayman and Bess is spoken in the two stanzas following the five dots. These stanzas are printed in italics. In your own words, explain what is different about them.

(17) What comments would you make about the love of Bess and the highwayman?

13. Strange Happenings

THE LESSON

Chaos ruled OK in the classroom
as bravely the teacher walked in
the havocwreakers ignored him
his voice was lost in the din

'The theme for today is violence
and homework will be set
I'm going to teach you a lesson
one that you'll never forget'

He picked on a boy who was shouting
and throttled him then and there
then garrotted the girl behind him
(the one with grotty hair)

Then sword in hand he hacked his way
between the chattering rows
'First come, first severed' he declared
'fingers, feet, or toes'

He threw the sword at a latecomer
it struck with deadly aim
then pulling out a shotgun
he continued with his game

The first blast cleared the backrow
(where those who skive hang out)
they collapsed like rubber dinghies
when the plug's pulled out

'Please may I leave the room sir?'
a trembling vandal enquired
'Of course you may' said teacher
put the gun to his temple and fired

The Head popped a head round the doorway
to see why a din was being made
nodded understandingly
then tossed in a grenade

And when the ammo was well spent
with blood on every chair
Silence shuffled forward
with its hands up in the air

The teacher surveyed the carnage
the dying and the dead
He waggled a finger severely
'Now let that be a lesson' he said

ROGER MCGOUGH

The Lesson — Concentrating on the poem

(1)   In the poem there are many examples of extreme violence. Write down a few of them.
(2)   The events in the poem are too incredible to be believed. Do you agree? Explain your viewpoint.
(3)   What are your feelings towards the teacher in the poem?
(4)   What is a vandal? Why was the vandal trembling?
(5)   The poem is arranged in stanzas of four lines. Write down the stanza you liked (a) best, and (b) least, and explain why.
(6)   Draw a picture showing what happens in one or two of the stanzas.
(7)   *Corporal* punishment is different from *capital* punishment. Try to explain the difference.
(8)   Explain the meanings of (a) throttled, (b) havocwreakers, (c) severed, (d) hacked.
(9)   The teacher said: 'I'm going to teach you a lesson
        one that you'll never forget'
Do you think he was successful? Why?
(10) 'The Lesson' is a very violent poem. Did you enjoy it? Why? What kind of poetry do you like? (Happy, or serious, or 'weird', or what?) Why?

What do you think?

(1) This poem is written from a teacher's viewpoint. What about the students' viewpoint? What do you think would happen if the students took over your school?

(2) Have you ever been in a classroom where there was chaos (extreme disorder)? Describe what happened.

(3) When there is a lot of noise in the classroom between lessons, and your teacher arrives, what happens?

(4) In your own life you probably will have witnessed violence of some kind. Briefly describe the experience in two or three sentences. Then read your description aloud to the class and compare it with the experiences of your friends.

(5) Some people think that our society is becoming more and more violent. Do you agree? Why?

(6) Do you believe that teachers have to punish students? Why? What are some of the punishments you dislike?

(7) Do you think that some of your teachers have a lot to put up with? Why?

This poem was written in the days of pounds, shillings and pence, before we changed to dollars and cents. Let's hope that Miss Strawberry's purse has not changed over to decimal currency.

MISS STRAWBERRY'S PURSE

Miss Strawberry has a long fat purse
To keep her money in.
It is a rare and handsome purse
Made of crocodile skin.
It is a crocodile skin without a doubt
For she did not take the crocodile out
And when she walks to town to shop
He follows behind her clop, clop-clop,
And opens his mouth and bellows aloud
And swishes his tail amongst the crowd.
Now and again there's an angry mutter
As a man is swept into the gutter.
When in a shop it is time to pay
Shopkeepers look at the brute in dismay
When Miss Strawberry says 'Crocky, open wide,'

And 'Shopman, if you can dodge his paws
And reach beyond those ugly jaws,
You'll find your money deep inside —
But I warn you if you make him cough
He'll probably bite your arm right off.'
The shopkeeper usually says 'No worry.
Pay next month. I'm in no hurry.'
But a grocer once, owed four-pounds-ten,
Said 'That's worth more than one of my men.'
He called his errand-boy, 'Hey, son,
Come over here, we'll have some fun,
I'll hold your legs and guard you while
You crawl in this quiet old crocodile
And collect in his vitals four-pounds-ten.
If you bring it out again
I'll give you sixpence for your trouble.
Come here, son, and at the double!'
Now the length of Miss Strawberry's crocodile's throat
Is four times as long as a shopman's coat.
The crocodile opened fearfully wide
And the errand-boy crawled right down inside.
When he had gathered four-pounds-ten
And hurriedly tried to back out again,
The crocodile closed his jaws with a smile,
Saying, 'One of the joys of a crocodile,
Indeed you might say, his favourite joy,
Is making a meal of a messenger-boy.'

ERIC C. ROLLS

Poet's Corner

Eric C. Rolls has explained his inspiration for 'Miss Strawberry's Purse':
'One day Kerry Jane, my daughter, who was walking about the verandah
in a strange manner, said "I wish she'd bring back my head. I can't
see where I'm going," and Kim her brother, who was hopping on one
foot, said "She's an awful old woman, isn't she? She's got my foot, too."
When I said "Who has?" they answered together "Miss Strawberry".'
The poet then went away, and within a few months he had written a
whole book of Miss Strawberry poems.

GEORGE AND THE DRAGONFLY

Georgie Jennings was spit almighty.
When the golly was good
he could down a dragonfly at 30 feet
and drown a 100 midges with the fallout.
At the drop of a cap
he would outspit lads
years older and twice his size.
Freckled and rather frail
he assumed the quiet dignity
beloved of schoolboy heroes.

But though a legend in his own playtime
Georgie Jennings failed miserably in the classroom
and left school at 15 to work for his father.
And talents such as spitting
are considered unbefitting
for upandcoming porkbutchers.

I haven't seen him since,
but like to imagine some summer soiree
when, after a day moistening mince,
George and his wife entertain tanned friends.
And after dinner, sherrytongued talk
drifts back to schooldays
the faces halfrecalled, the adventures
overexaggerated. And the next thing
that shy sharpshooter of days gone by
is led, vainly protesting, on to the lawn,
where, in the hush of a golden August evening
a reputation, 20 years tall, is put to the test.
So he takes extra care as yesterheroes must,
fires, and a dragonfly, incapsulated, bites the dust.
Then amidst bravos and tinkled applause,
blushing, Georgie leads them back indoors.

ROGER McGOUGH

Poet's Corner

'George and the Dragonfly' is based part on truth, part on fantasy. There was a boy I knew at school who was gifted like the one in the poem (although his targets were not confined to dragonflies, and I doubt if he grew to acquire a taste for sherry and suntanned friends). Everybody is good at something, and I suppose this poem is about children being good at things which society later deems unimportant. And I think it's a pity.

Roger McGough

George and the Dragonfly — Your analysis

(1) Georgie Jennings made a great impression on the poet when he was a boy. Why was this so?

(2) Why did Georgie Jennings seem to be a rather unlikely hero?

(3) Did Georgie tend to skite about his skills? Write down a line or two to support your answer.

(4) Why is it possible to feel sad for Georgie?

(5) What is the meaning of, 'And talents such as spitting
             are considered unbefitting
             for upandcoming porkbutchers.'?

(6) In what ways did you find this poem different from others you have studied? Did you enjoy it more than other poems? Why?

(7) Explain the meaning of:
     (a) 'sherrytongued talk';
     (b) 'that shy sharpshooter of days gone by';
     (c) 'a dragonfly, incapsulated, bites the dust'.

Discussion Points

• Not all of us can be talented. But generally there is something that we can do rather well. Describe something that *you* do well, and enjoy doing.

• Do you know of someone who has an unusual skill or hobby? Describe it to the class in a few sentences.

THE YARN OF THE NANCY BELL

'Twas on the shores that round our coast
  From Deal to Ramsgate span,
That I found alone on a piece of stone
  An elderly naval man.

His hair was weedy, his beard was long,
  And weedy and long was he.
And I heard this wight on the shore recite,
  In a singular minor key:

'Oh, I am a cook and the captain bold,
  And the mate of the *Nancy* brig,
And a bo'sun tight, and a midshipmite,
  And the crew of the captain's gig.'

And he shook his fist and he tore his hair,
  Till I really felt afraid,
For I couldn't help thinking the man had been drinking,
  And so I simply said:

'Oh, elderly man, it's little I know
  Of the duties of men of the sea,
And I'll eat my hand if I understand
  How you can possibly be

'At once a cook, and a captain bold,
  And the mate of the *Nancy* brig,
And a bo'sun tight, and a midshipmite,
  And the crew of the captain's gig.'

Then he gave a hitch to his trousers, which
  Is a trick all seamen larn,
And having got rid of a thumping quid,
  He spun this painful yarn:

' 'Twas in the good ship *Nancy Bell*
  That we sailed to the Indian sea,
And there on a reef we come to grief,
  Which has often occurred to me.

'And pretty nigh all the crew was drowned
  (There was seventy-seven o' soul),
And only ten of the *Nancy's* men
  Said "Here!" to the muster-roll.

'There was me and the cook and the captain bold,
  And the mate of the *Nancy's* brig,
And the bo'sun tight, and a midshipmite,
  And the crew of the captain's gig.

'For a month we'd neither wittles nor drink,
  'Till a-hungry we did feel,
So we drawed a lot, and accordin' shot
  The captain for our meal.

'The next lot fell to the *Nancy's* mate,
  And a delicate dish he made;
Then our appetite with the midshipmite
  We seven survivors stayed.

'And then we murdered the bo'sun tight,
  And he much resembled pig;
Then we wittled free, did the cook and me,
  On the crew of the captain's gig.

'Then only the cook and me was left,
  And the delicate question, "Which
Of us goes to the kettle?" arose,
  And we argued it out as sich.

'For I loved that cook as a brother, I did,
  And the cook he worshipped me;
But we'd both be blowed if we'd either be stowed
  In the other chap's hold, you see.

' "I'll be eat if you dines off me," says Tom.
  "Yes, that", says I, "you'll be—
I'm boiled if I die, my friend," quoth I.
  And "Exactly so," quoth he.

'Says he, "Dear James, to murder me
  Were a foolish thing to do,
For don't you see that you can't cook *me*.
  While I can — and will — cook *you*!"

'So he boils the water, and takes the salt
    And the pepper in portions true
(Which he never forgot) and some chopped shallot,
    And some sage and parsley too.

' "Come here," says he, with a proper pride,
    Which his smiling features tell,
" 'Twill soothing be if I let you see
    How extremely nice you'll smell."

'And he stirred it round and round and round,
    And he sniffed at the foaming froth;
When I ups with his heels, and smothers his squeals
    In the scum of the boiling broth.

'And I eat that cook in a week or less,
    And — as I eating be
The last of his chops, why, I almost drops,
    For a vessel in sight I see.

'And I never larf, and I never smile,
    And I never lark nor play,
But sit and croak, and a single joke
    I have — which is to say:

'Oh, I am a cook and a captain bold,
    And the mate of the *Nancy* brig,
And a bo'sun tight, and a midshipmite,
    And the crew of the captain's gig!'

W. S. GILBERT

The Yarn of the Nancy Bell — Some essential vocabulary

Some of the words in the poem, especially the naval ones, are a little unfamiliar. If you read the poem closely, however, you'll be able to match most of them (left list) with their meanings (right list) below.

Words	Meanings
wight	midshipman — an apprentice officer
midshipmite	lump or wad of chewing tobacco
gig	person, creature
quid	tale or story
wittles	ship
yarn	boatswain or petty officer
bo'sun	small boat provided with oars and sails
brig	food (victuals)

Reading for details

(1) Quote the two lines that tell us how many of the men of the *Nancy Bell* were left after the ship struck the reef.

(2) Who were these survivors?

(3) How many men were there in the captain's gig?

(4) What decision did the survivors make when they were absolutely starving?

(5) What happened to the captain of the *Nancy Bell*?

(6) Finally there were only two men left. Who were they?

(7) What argument did the cook give to support his claim that he should be the last man alive?

(8) How did the sailor telling the story make sure that he, and not the cook, was the sole survivor?

(9) What do you think is amusing about this poem? Is it the story, or is it something about the way it is told?

from COLONEL FAZACKERLEY

Colonel Fazackerley Butterworth-Toast
Bought an old castle complete with a ghost,
But someone or other forgot to declare
To Colonel Fazack that the spectre was there.

On the very first evening, while waiting to dine,
The Colonel was taking a fine sherry wine,
When the ghost, with a furious flash and a flare,
Shot out of the chimney and shivered, 'Beware!'

Colonel Fazackerley put down his glass
And said, 'My dear fellow, that's really first class!
I just can't conceive how you do it at all.
I imagine you're going to a Fancy Dress Ball?'

At this, the dread ghost gave a withering cry.
Said the Colonel (his monocle firm in his eye),
'Now just how you do it I wish I could think.
Do sit down and tell me, and please have a drink.'

The ghost in his phosphorus cloak gave a roar
And floated about between ceiling and floor.
He walked through a wall and returned through a pane
And backed up the chimney and came down again.

Said the Colonel, 'With laughter I'm feeling quite weak!'
(As trickles of merriment ran down his cheek).
My house-warming party I hope you won't spurn.
You *must* say you'll come and you'll give us a turn!'

At this, the poor spectre — quite out of his wits —
Proceeded to shake himself almost to bits.
He rattled his chains and he clattered his bones
And he filled the whole castle with mumbles and moans.

But Colonel Fazackerley, just as before,
Was simply delighted and called out, 'Encore!'
At which the ghost vanished, his efforts in vain,
And never was seen at the castle again.

'Oh dear, what a pity!' said Colonel Fazack.
'I don't know his name, so I won't call him back.'
And then with a smile that was hard to define,
Colonel Fazackerley went in to dine.

CHARLES CAUSLEY

Colonel Fazackerley — Think about the ending

Why was the Colonel's smile 'hard to define'? Was he satisfied at the end, or not? Explain your answer.

Acting it out

A good way to enhance the humour of this poem is to have it acted out in your classroom. Have someone playing the part of, and saying the words spoken by, the Colonel; and have someone else imaginatively acting out the ghost's role. Weave the action and the Colonel's words together by using the whole class (or a section of the class) as the 'Narrator' reciting the poem.

Let your imagination go, and see what you come up with!

SIR SMASHAM UPPE

Good afternoon, Sir Smasham Uppe!
We're having tea: do take a cup!
Sugar and milk? Now let me see —
Two lumps, I think? ... Good gracious me!
The silly thing slipped off your knee!
Pray don't apologise, old chap:
A very trivial mishap!
So clumsy of you? How absurd!
My dear Sir Smasham, not a word!
Now do sit down and have another,
And tell us all about your brother —
You know, the one who broke his head.
Is the poor fellow still in bed?
A chair — allow me sir! ... Great Scott!
That *was* a nasty smash! Eh, what?
Oh, not at all: the chair was old —
Queen Anne, or so we have been told.
We've got at least a dozen more:
Just leave the pieces on the floor.
I want you to admire our view:
Come nearer to the window, do;
And look how beautiful ... Tut, tut!
You didn't see that it was shut?
I hope you are not badly cut!
Not hurt? A fortunate escape!

Amazing! Not a single scrape!
And now, if you have finished tea,
I fancy you might like to see
A little thing or two I've got.
That china plate? Yes, worth a lot:
A beauty too ... Ah, there it goes!
I trust it didn't hurt your toes?
Your elbow brushed it off the shelf?
Of course: I've done the same myself.
And now, my dear Sir Smasham — oh,
You surely don't intend to go?
You *must* be off? Well, come again.
So glad you're fond of porcelain!

E. V. RIEU

Sir Smasham Uppe — Two questions

(1)   How does the host *appear* to feel about Sir Smasham?

(2)   How does Sir Smasham feel about all his accidents?

Sir Smasham isn't the only one with this particular problem!

14. Alliteration

Alliteration is the commencing of two or more words close together with the same letter (or sound). Sometimes the repeated sound does the job of getting our attention; sometimes it adds a harsh note, a soft note, an enchanted note. Often, alliteration goes hand in hand with meaning. (Note: alliteration involves *consonant* and not *vowel* sounds).

Examples of alliteration
- *A*round the *r*ugged *r*ocks, the *r*agged *r*ascal *r*an.
- Out of the *d*ying *d*arkness, over the forest *d*im,
  The pearly *d*ew of the *d*awning clung to each giant limb.
- *F*ull *f*athom *f*ive thy *f*ather lies.
- Over the *c*obbles he *cl*attered and *cl*ashed in the dark inn-yard.
  (*Notice the onomatopoeia as well as the alliteration in this line.*)
- I am cold and alone,
  On my tree root *s*itting as *st*ill as *st*one.
- *Sh*eila is *s*elling her *sh*op at the *s*ea*sh*ore
  But *sh*ops at the *s*ea*sh*ore are *s*ure hard to *s*ell.

Alliteration in the Comic Strips

Both of the following comic strips contain examples of alliteration. Write down the appropriate words and underline the letters being alliterated.

Tongue-Twisting

Here's a real tongue-twister of a poem for you. Try saying it to yourself. Do you know why it is so hard to say? Yes, it's the alliteration of the letter 'b'.

BETTY BOTTER

Betty Botter bought some butter,
But, she said, the butter's bitter;
If I put it in my batter
It will make my batter bitter,
But a bit of better butter's
Bound to make my batter better.
So she bought a bit of butter
Better than her bitter butter,
And she put it in her batter
And the batter wasn't bitter.
So 'twas better Betty Botter
Bought a bit of better butter.

ANONYMOUS

Alliteration in Poetry and Speech

Poets often use alliteration to create all kinds of effects, feelings, moods and movements. But many of our everyday phrases and expressions also employ alliteration. Let's examine both of these aspects.

Find the alliteration

Look at this list of 20 quotations collected from a wide range of popular poems. Write them down and underline the examples of alliteration.

(1) I have seen old ships sail like swans asleep.

(2) Not a drum was heard, not a funeral note.

(3) He clasps the crag with crooked hands;
    Close to the sun in lonely lands.

(4) The Assyrian came down like the wolf on the fold.

(5) I sprang to the stirrup, and Joris, and he.

(6) Only the stuttering rifles' rapid rattle.

(7) But crackle-dry as wing of dragonfly.

(8) Take the big roller's shoulder, speed and swerve,
    Come to the long beach home like a gull diving.

(9) Its quick soft silver bell beating, beating.

(10) My love is like a red, red rose.

(11) Glory be to God for dappled things.

(12) Blow, bugle, blow, set the wild echoes flying.

(13) A score of troopers were scattering wide
     And a hundred more were ready to ride.

(14) 'Who touches a hair of yon head
     Dies like a dog! March on!' he said.

(15) Water, water, everywhere,
     Nor any drop to drink.

(16) The Lotus blooms below the barren peak.

(17) The league-long roller thundering on the reef.

(18) When men were all asleep the snow came flying.

(19) Eyes full of sparkling wickedness, ears finely cut, flexibly moving.

(20) The Miller was a chap of sixteen stone,
     A great stout fellow big in brawn and bone.

Complete the common couples

There are quite a few well-known alliteration couples — e.g. *l*ife and *l*imb, *h*ouse and *h*ome, and so on. See whether you can supply the missing partner for each of the following.

spick and ....

.... and sound

thick and ....

.... and proper

rough and ....

.... and don'ts

fast and ....

.... and turn

hale and ....

.... and that

sweet and ....

.... and roll

rant and ....

.... and tested

wild and ....

.... and hers

wash and ....

.... and cheese

black and ....

.... and steady

home and ....

.... and bred

sticks and ....

.... and dash

tried and ....

.... and stripes

pots and ....

.... and slide

birds and ....

.... and spice

trials and ....

.... and baggage

15. Poems to Compare

'The Last of His Tribe' and 'Then and Now' are both concerned with the passing of time. In the first of the two poems, the Aboriginal warrior thinks back to the happy life he had with his wife and tribe, who have perished. In the second, Aboriginal poet Kath Walker is pointing out that the Aborigines were far happier in the past, before they became exposed to the white man's way of life.

THE LAST OF HIS TRIBE

He crouches and buries his face on his knees,
 And hides in the dark of his hair;
For he cannot look up to the storm-smitten trees,
 Or think of the loneliness there —
 Of the loss and the loneliness there.

The wallaroos grope through the tufts of the grass,
 And turn to their coverts for fear;
But he sits in the ashes and lets them pass
 Where the boomerangs sleep with the spear —
 With the nullah, the sling, and the spear.

Uloola, behold him! The thunder that breaks
 On the tops of the rocks with the rain,
And the wind which drives up with the salt of the lakes,
 Have made him a hunter again —
 A hunter and fisher again.

For his eyes have been full with a smouldering thought;
 But he dreams of the hunts of yore,
And of foes that he sought, and of fights that he fought
 With those who will battle no more —
 Who will go to the battle no more.

It is well that the water which tumbles and fills
  Goes moaning and moaning along;
For an echo rolls out from the sides of the hills,
  And he starts at a wonderful song —
  At the sound of a wonderful song.

And he sees through the rents of the scattering fogs
  The corroboree warlike and grim,
And the lubra who sat by the fire on the logs,
  To watch, like a mourner, for him —
  Like a mother and mourner for him.

Will he go in his sleep from these desolate lands,
  Like a chief, to the rest of his race,
With the honey-voiced woman who beckons and stands,
  And gleams like a dream in his face —
  Like a marvellous dream in his face?

HENRY KENDALL

The Last of His Tribe — Feelings

Draw up the table and see whether you can find phrases and sentences from the poem to match up with the feelings listed.

Feelings	Phrases and Sentences
Despair	
Fear	
Happiness	
Sadness	
Loneliness	

from THEN AND NOW

In my dreams I hear my tribe
Laughing as they hunt and swim,
But dreams are shattered by rushing car,
By grinding tram and hissing train,
And I see no more my tribe of old
As I walk alone in the teeming town.

I have seen corroboree
Where that factory belches smoke;
Here where they have memorial park
One time lubras dug for yams;
One time our dark children played
There where the railway yards are now,
And where I remember the didgeridoo
Calling us to dance and play,
Offices now, neon lights now,
Bank and shop and advertisement now,
Traffic and trade of the busy town.

No more woomera, no more boomerang,
No more play about, no more the old ways,
Children of nature we were then,
No clocks hurrying crowds to toil.
Now I am civilised and work in the white way,
Now I have dress, now I have shoes;
Isn't she lucky to have a good job!
Better when I had only a dillybag.
Better when I had nothing but happiness.

KATH WALKER

Then and Now — Facts

By referring to 'Then and Now', complete the table. The first one has been done to help you.

Then	Now
corroboree	factory belches smoke
lubras dug for yams	
dark children played here	
the didgeridoo calling us to dance and play	
better when I had only a dillybag	

The subject of mosquitoes is a popular one with poets. Can you suggest why? While you're thinking about it, here are two mosquito poems for you to compare.

MOSQUITOES

Mosquitoes are blood relations
They doze on the white ceiling
Like the children upstairs
While we wake below

We are their livelihood
They wish us no harm
Stealing through windows
With their fine instruments
And teething drone
There they say you hardly felt it

And they work like surgeons
While we stir in sleep
Tapping veins adjusting
The flow dim
Figures at work murmuring
Creatures of the subconscious

Extinct cloaked vampires
Spirits hooked on blood
Live scarlet drops
Hanging like fruit bats
From the ceiling — our babies
Our own flesh and blood
Loving us and jealous
Mmmmmm they cry at dusk
They are helpless without us.

DAVID CAMPBELL

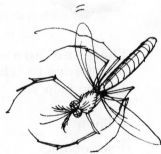

Mosquitoes — One view

(1) Why does David Campbell refer to mosquitoes as 'blood relations'?
(2) How are the mosquitoes 'like surgeons'?
(3) 'Live scarlet drops' — When are mosquitoes like this?
(4) 'From the ceiling — our babies' seems an incredible statement. Can you suggest why the poet calls the mosquitoes 'our babies'?

(5) What do vampires do? Do you think the poet is justified in referring to the mosquitoes as vampires?

(6) Why are mosquitoes 'helpless without us'?

MOSQUITO

On the fine wire of his whine he walked,
Unseen in the ominous bedroom dark.
A traitor to his camouflage, he talked
A thirsty blue streak distinct as a spark.

I was to him a fragrant lake of blood
From which he had to sip a drop or die.
A reservoir, a lavish field of food,
I lay awake, unconscious of size.

We seemed fair-matched opponents. Soft he dropped
Down like an anchor on his thread of song.
His nose sank thankfully in; then I slapped
At the sting on my arm, cunning and strong.

A cunning, strong Gargantua, I struck
When he was pinned in the feast of my flesh,
Lulled by my blood, relaxed, half-sated, stuck,
Engrossed in the gross rivers of myself.

Success! Without a cry the creature died,
Became a fleck of fluff upon the sheet.
The small welt of remorse subsides as side
By side we, murderer and murdered, sleep.

JOHN UPDIKE

Mosquito — Another view

(1) Explain why the mosquito was a 'traitor to his camouflage'.

(2) Find a line in the first stanza that reminds you of the *sound* a mosquito makes.

(3) Explain what the poet means by the simile, 'Down like an anchor on his thread of song.'

(4) In what way is the person in this poem 'cunning'?

(5) Who are the 'murderer' and 'murdered' in the last line? How does their 'sleep' differ?

(6) Which poem about mosquitoes did you prefer — David Campbell's or John Updike's? Can you explain why?

It has been suggested that Robert Browning wrote this poem while on board a ship travelling to Italy. The up-and-down motion of the waves supposedly brought to Browning's mind the movement of a horse galloping along.

The town of Ghent is in Belgium and Aix-la-Chapelle is just over the border in France. But there is no historical evidence for the events of the poem. Moreover, the distance between the two towns is more than fifty miles, which seems rather far for any horse to gallop at the pace that would have been required.

The poem owes much of its success to its rhythmic beat. When you read it aloud you can almost feel yourself riding along at great speed on one of the horses.

HOW THEY BROUGHT THE GOOD NEWS FROM GHENT TO AIX

[16—]

I sprang to the stirrup, and Joris, and he;
I galloped, Dirck galloped, we galloped all three;
'Good speed!' cried the watch, as the gate-bolts undrew;
'Speed!' echoed the wall to us galloping through;
Behind shut the postern,[1] the lights sank to rest,
And into the midnight we galloped abreast.

Not a word to each other; we kept the great pace
Neck by neck, stride by stride, never changing our place;
I turned in my saddle and made its girths tight,
Then shortened each stirrup, and set the pique[2] right,
Rebuckled the cheek-strap, chained slacker the bit,
Nor galloped less steadily Roland a whit.

1 *postern:* a small (back) gate.
2 *pique:* usually 'peak' — the highest part of the saddle-bow.

'Twas moonset at starting; but while we drew near
Lokeren, the cocks crew and twilight dawned clear;
At Boom, a great yellow star came out to see;
At Düffeld, 'twas morning as plain as could be;
And from the Mecheln church-steeple we heard the half-chime,
So Joris broke silence with, 'Yet there is time!'

At Aerschot, up leaped of a sudden the sun,
And against him the cattle stood black every one,
To stare thro' the mist at us galloping past,
And I saw my stout galloper Roland at last,
With resolute shoulders, each butting away
The haze, as some bluff river headland its spray.

And his low head and crest, just one sharp ear bent back
For my voice, and the other pricked out on his track;
And one eye's black intelligence, — ever that glance
O'er its white edge at me, his own master, askance!³
And the thick heavy spume-flakes which aye and anon⁴
His fierce lips shook upwards in galloping on.

By Hasselt, Dirck groaned; and cried Joris, 'Stay spur!
Your Roos galloped bravely, the fault's not in her,
We'll remember at Aix' — for one heard the quick wheeze
Of her chest, saw the stretched neck and staggering knees,
And sunk tail, and horrible heave of the flank,
As down on her haunches she shuddered and sank.

So we were left galloping, Joris and I,
Past Looz and past Tongres, no cloud in the sky;
The broad sun above laughed a pitiless laugh,
'Neath our feet broke the brittle bright stubble like chaff;
Till over by Dalhem a dome-spire sprang white,
And 'Gallop,' gasped Joris, 'for Aix is in sight!'

'How they'll greet us!' — and all in a moment his roan
Rolled neck and croup⁵ over, lay dead as a stone;
And there was my Roland to bear the whole weight
Of the news which alone could save Aix from her fate,
With his nostrils like pits full of blood to the brim,
And with circles of red for his eye-sockets' rim.

3 *askance:* sideways, i.e. out of the corner of his eye.
4 *aye and anon:* frequently, constantly.
5 *croup:* the rump of a horse. To 'roll over neck and croup' means to
    tumble over completely.

Then I cast loose my buffcoat, each holster let fall,
Shook off both my jack-boots, let go belt and all,
Stood up in the stirrup, leaned, patted his ear,
Called my Roland his pet-name, my horse without peer;
Clapped my hands, laughed and sang, any noise, bad or good,
Till at length into Aix Roland galloped and stood.

And all I remember is, friends flocking round
As I sat with his head 'twixt my knees on the ground;
And no voice but was praising this Roland of mine,
As I poured down his throat our last measure of wine,
Which (the burgesses voted by common consent)
Was no more than his due who brought good news from Ghent.

ROBERT BROWNING

The next poem is a parody of 'How They Brought the Good News from Ghent to Aix'. What is a parody? A parody imitates the characteristics of an original (poem, song, voice, etc) in order to make it appear ridiculous, while making the parody itself appear clever, funny and perhaps effective in conveying a message of some sort. Notice that the Yeatman and Sellar poem has rhythm and rhyme patterns similar to those of the Browning poem. However, the original was serious and dramatic, describing the saving of Aix from a great catastrophe; whereas the parody is full of ridiculous and farcical happenings.

from HOW I BROUGHT THE GOOD NEWS FROM AIX
TO GHENT (OR VICE VERSA)

I sprang to the rollocks and Jorrocks and me,
And I galloped, you galloped, he galloped, we galloped all three . . .
Not a word to each other; we kept changing place,
Neck to neck, back to front, ear to ear, face to face;
And we yelled once or twice, when we heard a clock chime,
'Would you kindly oblige us, *Is that the right time?*'
As I galloped, you galloped, he galloped, we galloped, ye galloped, they
   two shall have galloped; *let us trot.*

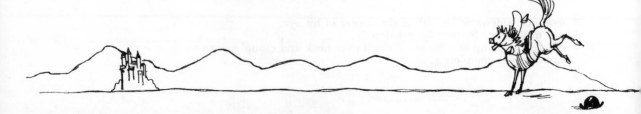

I unsaddled the saddle, unbuckled the bit,
Unshackled the bridle (the thing didn't fit)
And ungalloped, ungalloped, ungalloped, ungalloped a bit.
Then I cast off my bluff-coat, let my bowler hat fall,
Took off both my boots and my trousers and all —
Drank off my stirrup-cup, felt a bit tight,
And unbridled the saddle: it still wasn't right.

Then all I remember is, things reeling round
As I sat with my head 'twixt my ears on the ground —
For imagine my shame when they asked what I meant
And I had to confess that I'd been, gone and went
And *forgotten the news* I was bringing to Ghent,
Though I'd galloped and galloped and galloped and galloped and
    galloped
And galloped and galloped and galloped. (Had I not would have been
    galloped?)

Envoi

So I sprang to a taxi and shouted 'To Aix!'
And he blew on his horn and he threw off his brakes,
And all the way back till my money was spent
We rattled and rattled and rattled and rattled and rattled
And rattled and rattled —
And eventually sent a telegram.

                                R. J. YEATMAN and W. C. SELLAR

Bringing the Good News — Pick the parody

Copy down the following lines from Browning's poem, then match them up with the corresponding humorous lines from the Yeatman and Sellar poem.

Browning	Yeatman and Sellar
(1) We kept the great pace	
(2) 'Yet there is time!'	
(3) chained slacker the bit	
(4) Then I cast loose my buffcoat, each holster let fall	
(5) Shook off both my jack-boots, let go belt and all	
(6) As I sat with his head 'twixt my knees on the ground	

Here are two poems about snakes. The two poets take a very different approach to their subject. Their reasons for having written the poems make interesting reading.

SNAKE

Suddenly the grass before my feet
shakes and becomes alive.
The snake
twists, almost leaps,
graceful even in terror,
smoothness looping back over smoothness,
slithers away, disappears.
And the grass is again still.

And surely, by whatever means of communication
is available to snakes,
the word is passed:
Hey, I just met a man, a monster, too;
Must have been, oh, seven feet tall
So keep away from the long grass,
it's dangerous there.

IAN MUDIE

Poet's Corner

I met the snake at Sellicks Beach (South Australia). It was only a small one. When the man I was with started telling everyone to keep away from the long grass as there was a big snake there I began to wonder what the snake was thinking. That night I wrote the poem.

Ian Mudie

THE KILLER

The day was clear as fire,
the birds sang frail as glass,
when thirsty I came to the creek
and fell by its side in the grass.

My breast on the bright moss
and shower-embroidered weeds,
my lips to the live water
I saw him turn in the reeds.

Black horror sprang from the dark
in a violent birth,
and through its cloth of grass
I felt the clutch of earth.

O beat him into the ground.
O strike him till he dies —
or else your life itself
drains through those colourless eyes.

I struck again and again.
Slender in black and red
he lies, and his icy glance
turns outward, clear and dead.

But nimble my enemy
as water is, or wind.
He has slipped from his death aside
and vanished into my mind.

He has vanished whence he came,
my nimble enemy;
and the ants come out to the snake
and drink at his shallow eye.

JUDITH WRIGHT

Poet's Corner

I had not realised that my fear came from inside me and was not solved
by killing the snake, but would stay inside me and might lead to my
killing other innocent creatures — that, in fact, my fear was my enemy,
and not the snake at all. ... The poem was a way of making myself
realise that fear is what must be conquered, not anything in the outside
world that makes us afraid.

Judith Wright

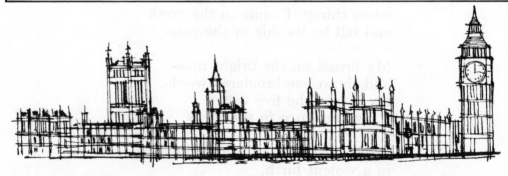

William Wordsworth, on 31 July 1802, was so excited, delighted and
enthralled by the sight of the city that he wrote a poem that very day to
show the depth of his feelings.

On the other hand, a modern poet — Murray Jennings — was so disgusted
with the view of Sydney from Pyrmont Bridge that he wrote a poem con-
demning what he saw. In doing this, he was obviously very mindful of
Wordsworth's original.

UPON WESTMINSTER BRIDGE

Earth has not anything to show more fair:
Dull would he be of soul who could pass by
A sight so touching in its majesty:
This City now doth, like a garment, wear
The beauty of the morning; silent, bare,
Ships, towers, domes, theatres, and temples lie
Open unto the fields, and to the sky;
All bright and glittering in the smokeless air.
Never did sun more beautifully steep
In his first splendour, valley, rock, or hill;
Ne'er saw I, never felt, a calm so deep!
The river glideth at his own sweet will:
Dear God! the very houses seem asleep;
And all that mighty heart is lying still!

WILLIAM WORDSWORTH

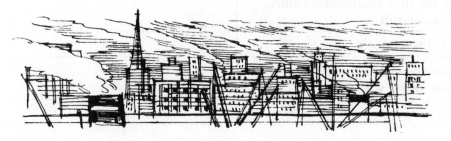

UPON PYRMONT BRIDGE

Earth has not anything to show less fair:
Dulled are we-of-the-soul who do pass by
A sight so touching in its tragedy:
This City now does like a garment wear
The hot breath of the morning traffic there;
Ships, towers, domes, theatres, and plazas lie
Open unto the fumes that hang in the sky;
All blanched and jaundiced in the smog-filled air.
Never did sun more encumbered steep
In his first grey-brown halo, old, and chill;
Ne'er saw I, never felt, a panic so deep!
The harbour chokes now in its own sour fill;
Dear God! the very buildings stand as cheap
Reminders of that mighty heart soon lying still!

MURRAY JENNINGS

Upon Two Bridges — Positives and negatives

In the left-hand column, words and phrases from 'Upon Westminster Bridge' have been set out. All of them have *positive* associations. See whether you can insert, next to them, the corresponding words and phrases from 'Upon Pyrmont Bridge', with their *negative* associations. The first one has been done to help you.

'Upon Westminster Bridge'	'Upon Pyrmont Bridge'
more fair	less fair
majesty	
The beauty of the morning	
Open unto the fields, and to the sky	
All bright and glittering in the smokeless air	
In his first splendour, valley, rock, or hill	
a calm so deep!	
The river glideth at his own sweet will	
the very houses seem asleep	

Did you get the impression that certain things have changed since 1802?

16. Personification

In literature, and particularly in poetry, some *things* are often considered as if they were alive, although they in fact are not. Look carefully at these examples.

- The headlights winked in the gathering dusk.
- Gentle breezes stroked our faces.
- Fire walked across the hill.

The headlights, breezes and fire have taken on *human* qualities. This is **personification**, the giving of living qualities such as habits, actions, feelings — even *personalities* — to non-living things.

Read through the poem 'The Frowning Cliff'.

THE FROWNING CLIFF

The sea has a laugh
And the cliff a frown;
For the laugh of the sea
Is wearing him down.

Lipping and lapping
Frown as he may,
The laughing sea
Will eat him away;

Knees and body,
And tawny head,
He'll smile at last
On a golden bed.

HERBERT ASQUITH

The Frowning Cliff — Think, write and draw

(1) What human qualities is the sea given in this poem?
(2) What human characteristics is the cliff given?

(3) Why does the sea have a laugh?

(4) Why is the poem called 'The Frowning Cliff?'

(5) Try to explain what the last stanza is suggesting will happen.

(6) Draw a picture in which you give human qualities to the sea and the cliff.

Here is another poem. This time a watch is being personified.

THE WATCH

When I
took my
watch to the watchfixer I
felt privileged but also pained to watch the operation. He
had long fingernails and a voluntary squint. He
fixed a magnifying cup over his
squint eye. He
undressed my
watch. I
watched him
split her
in three layers and lay her
middle — a quivering viscera — in a circle on a little plinth. He
shoved shirt sleeves up and leaned like an ogre over my
naked watch. With critical pincers he
poked and stirred. He
lifted out little private things with a magnet too tiny for me
to watch almost. 'Watch out!' I
almost said. His
eye watched, enlarged, the secrets of my
watch, and I
watched anxiously. Because what if he
touched her
ticker too rough, and she
gave up the ghost out of pure fright? Or put her
things back backwards so she'd
run backwards after this? Or he
might lose a minuscule part, connected to her
exquisite heart, and mix her
up, instead of fix her.

And all the time,
all the time-
pieces on the walls, on the shelves, told the time,
told the time
in swishes and ticks,
swishes and ticks,
and seemed to be gloating, as they watched and told. I
felt faint, I
was about to lose my breath — my
ticker going lickety-split — when watchfixer clipped her
three slices together with a gleam and two flicks of his
tools like chopsticks. He
spat out his
eye, lifted her
high, gave her
a twist, set her
hands right, and laid her
little face, quite as usual, in its place on my
wrist.

MAY SWENSON

The Watch — Four questions and a sketch
(1) What words tell you that the watch is female?
(2) The word 'operation' suggests that the watch is human. What word or words would normally be used in place of 'operation'?
(3) The watchmaker opens up the watch, and the poet continues with the personification. Find as many human terms as you can that are applied to the inner mechanism of the watch.
(4) Even the other timepieces on the wall are personified. What words show you this?
(5) Draw a picture of the watch in its personified state.

More examples of personification

Here are some further examples of personification. Explain how each of the words in heavy type is personified (given human qualities).

(1) The **sun** peeped over the window-sill.
(2) **Stars** winked in the heavens.
(3) The **trees** sighed.
(4) The **river** moaned.
(5) The **fog** crept up from the sea.
(6) The **wind** howled around the house.
(7) The **brook** chattered over the stones.
(8) **Leaves** danced in the breeze.
(9) The **tree-tops** kissed.
(10) Softly sing the **waters**.
(11) The **flames** of the bushfire raced across the hill.
(12) The old **door-hinge** groaned.

SPURT

NO GOOD WILL EVER COME OF THAT STUFF!

17. Feelings

STUFF

Lovers lie around in it
Broken glass is found in it
Grass
I like that stuff

Tuna fish get trapped in it
Legs come wrapped in it
Nylon
I like that stuff

Eskimos and tramps chew it
Madame Tussaud gave status to it
Wax
I like that stuff

Elephants get sprayed with it
Scotch is made with it
Water
I like that stuff

Clergy are dumbfounded by it
Bones are surrounded by it
Flesh
I like that stuff

Harps are strung with it
Mattresses are sprung with it
Wire
I like that stuff

Carpenters make cots of it
Undertakers use lots of it
Wood
I like that stuff

Cigarettes are lit by it
Pensioners get happy when they sit by it
Fire
I like that stuff

Dankworth's alto is made of it, most of it
Scoobdedoo is composed of it
Plastic
I like that stuff

Man made fibres and raw materials
Old rolled gold and breakfast cereals
Platinum linoleum
I like that stuff

Skin on my hands
Hair on my head
Toenails on my feet
And linen on my bed

Well I like that stuff
Yes I like that stuff
The earth
Is made of earth
And I like that stuff.

ADRIAN MITCHELL

Stuff — About the poem

This is a simple poem — a poem of celebration. The poet is celebrating the
'stuff' of life — the materials out of which are made things that he enjoys.
Because he enjoys the end-product (for example, the cool jazz of John Dank-
worth's alto saxophone) he celebrates the 'stuff' out of which it is made —
plastic.

Try your hand

What are some of the things *you* like in life? What materials are they made
of? Write a celebratory poem in which you honour the 'stuff' of which these
things you enjoy are made.

CLOTHES

My mother keeps telling me
When she was in her teens
She wore quite different clothes from mine
And hadn't heard of jeans,

T-shirts, no hats, and dresses that
Reach far above our knees.
I laughed at first and then I thought
One day my kids will tease

And scoff at what *I'm* wearing now.
What will *their* fashions be?
I'd give an awful lot to know,
To look ahead and see.

Girls dressed like girls perhaps once more
And boys no longer half
Resembling us. Oh, what's in store
To make *our* children laugh?

ELIZABETH JENNINGS

Clothes — Getting behind the poem

(1) Why do you think the girl's mother *keeps* telling her how girls' clothing used to be quite different?

(2) How do you think the mother feels about her daughter's clothes?

(3) What is it that causes the girl to stop laughing at her mother's words?

(4) What is it that the poet would 'give an awful lot to know'?

(5) 'Girls dressed like girls perhaps once more', writes the poet. She seems to have some fixed ideas about what girls should wear. How do you think she imagines that a girl dressed like a girl would look?

(6) What things is she speaking of when she refers to boys 'half resembling' girls?

(7) Why does she expect that children in future years will laugh at *her* fashions?

(8) In one or two sentences explain the *theme* of this poem — the message the poet wants to convey.

Sometimes it's hard to imagine people involved in activities other than the ones in which we are accustomed to seeing them. It may be hard to imagine a bank manager riding a trail-bike, or an insurance salesman out hang-gliding. This poem describes the reaction of a person upon hearing that his teacher has a go at fishing.

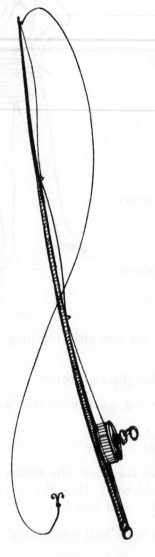

HE DON'T KNOW THE *INSIDE* FEEL

My teacher fish!
You must be screwed up, man.
A teacher? Hell
A teacher TEACHES.
He don't know the outdoor stuff.
He don't care.
He'd never walk by himself
Before breakfast
Across fields
Gettin his feet soaked
Just to fish!
He's a teacher.
He teaches.

He marks papers
Or he reads books.
He don't fish with no 2-ounce rod
And lay that long line easy on the top
Like this here . . . Look!
Oh, man
Don't tell me he hears them wild birds.
He don't.
He don't know the *inside* feel
Of white water rushin
Cold against his knees.
He don't know fishin, man.
Not like me.

HERBERT R. ADAMS

Getting inside
(1)   How does this person feel about his teacher?
(2)   (i)   Find *an action* that the poet thinks his teacher couldn't ever
            carry out.
      (ii) Find *a sound* that he feels his teacher wouldn't have heard.

(iii) Find *a feeling* that he doesn't believe his teacher has experienced.

(3) This person believes that fishing is something special. Why? What does it really mean to him.

Remember what it was like on *your* first day at a new school? Here's one person's description of the experience.

THE NEW BOY

The door swung inward. I stood and breathed
The new-school atmosphere.
The smell of polish and disinfectant,
And the flavour of my own fear.

I followed into the cloakroom; the walls
Rang to the shattering noise
Of boys who barged and boys who banged;
Boys and still more boys!

A boot flew by me. Its angry owner
Pursued with force and yell;
Somewhere a man snapped orders; somewhere
There clanged a warning bell.

And there I hung with my new schoolmates;
They pushing and shoving me; I
Unknown, unwanted, pinned to the wall;
On the verge of ready-to-cry.

Then, from the doorway, a boy called out:
'Hey, you over there! You're new!
Don't just stand there propping the wall up!
I'll look after you!'

I turned; I timidly raised my eyes;
He stood and grinned meanwhile;
And my fear died, and my lips answered
Smile for his smile.

He showed me the basins, the rows of pegs;
He hung my cap at the end;
He led me away to my new classroom ...
And now that boy's my friend.

                                          JOHN WALSH

The New Boy — Understanding

(1)   What are three things the new boy notices when he first enters the school?

(2)   What causes the new boy to be 'pinned to the wall'?

(3)   What sort of boy does he appear to be?

(4)   From what he says, what sort of person does the boy who 'called out' seem to be?

(5)   What is the effect of the 'old' boy's smile on the new boy?

Appreciating

(6)   The first sentence is short. What effect is thus achieved?

(7)   What is the effect of the line, 'On the verge of ready-to-cry.'?

(8)   The poet has sought to re-create certain emotions with his poem. What are they? As far as you're concerned, has he succeeded?

Discussion Point

Organise a class discussion on 'The Problems of Fitting into a New School'. List the problems and discuss ways of overcoming them. If any suggestions seem particularly worthwhile you might be able to pass them on through your School Council.

ROUGH

My parents kept me from children who were rough
Who threw words like stones and who wore torn clothes.
Their thighs showed through rags. They ran in the street
And climbed cliffs and stripped by the country streams.

I feared more than tigers their muscles like iron
Their jerking hands and their knees tight on my arms.
I feared the salt coarse pointing of those boys
Who copied my lisp behind me on the road.

They were lithe, they sprang out behind hedges
Like dogs to bark at my world. They threw mud
While I looked the other way, pretending to smile.
I longed to forgive them, but they never smiled.

STEPHEN SPENDER

Rough — Analysing feelings

(1)   What did the poet's parents fear about contact between their son and the 'rough' children?

(2) How did the poet feel about the rough children? Upon what evidence do you base your view?

(3) How did the rough children feel about Stephen Spender? How did they show their feelings?

(4) What action of the rough ones made Spender feel locked out of their world?

(5) What feelings are aroused in you towards
    (i)   Spender?
    (ii)   the rough children?
How does the poet arouse these feelings?

ONE SUMMER

One summer you
aeroplaned away,
too much money
away for me, and
stayed there for
quite a few
missed embraces.

Before leaving
you smiled me that
you'd return all of
a mystery moment and
would airletter me
every few breakfasts
in the meantime.
           This
you did, and I thank
you most kissingly.
              I
wish however, that I
could hijackerplane
to the Ignited States
of Neon where I'd
crash land perfectly
in the deserted
airport of your heart.

STEVE TURNER

One Summer — Unusual use of language

This poem contains many examples of unusual use of language. Instead of using *ordinary* words and phrases, the poet uses *fresh* words and phrases. Their interest-level is higher, and frequently they compress language and 'save' words.

Look at the following table and you will see an example of this. 'Aeroplaned away' is a fresh way of saying 'flew away in an aeroplane'. Draw up the table in your exercise book and work out an ordinary way of expressing each of the 'fresh' phrases or words from the poem.

Poet's 'fresh' phrase	An 'ordinary' way of saying it
(1) 'aeroplaned away'	flew away in an aeroplane
(2) 'too much money away'	
(3) 'for quite a few missed embraces'	
(4) 'you smiled me'	
(5) 'you'd return all of a mystery moment'	
(6) 'airletter me'	
(7) 'every few breakfasts in the meantime'	
(8) 'I thank you most kissingly'	
(9) 'hijackerplane'	
(10) 'Ignited States of Neon'	
(11) 'where I'd crash land perfectly'	

Ideally the humorous poetry of Pam Ayres should be read aloud, so get one of your good class-readers (someone who's a bit of an actor or actress) to read for the class.

OH NO, I GOT A COLD

I am sitting on the sofa,
By the fire and staying in,
Me head is free of comfort
And me nose is free of skin.
Me friends have run for cover,
They have left me pale and sick
With me pockets full of tissues
And me nostrils full of Vick.

That bloke in the telly adverts,
He's supposed to have a cold,
He has a swig of whatnot
And he drops off, good as gold,
His face like snowing harvest
Slips into sweet repose,
Well, I bet this tortured breathing
Never whistled down his nose.

I burnt me bit of dinner
Cause I've lost me sense of smell,
But then, I couldn't taste it,
So that worked out very well.
I'd buy some, down the café,
But I know that at the till,
A voice from work will softly say
'I thought that you were ill'.

So I'm wrapped up in a blanket
With me feet up on a stool,
I've watched the telly programmes
And the kids come home from school,
But what I haven't watched for
Is any sympathy,
Cause all you ever get is:
'Oh no, keep away from me!'

Medicinal discovery,
It moves in mighty leaps,
It leapt straight past the common cold
And gave it us for keeps.
Now I'm not a fussy woman,
There's no malice in me eye
But I wish that they could cure
the common cold. That's all. Goodbye.

PAM AYRES

Analysing the humour of Pam Ayres

Look at each of the following aspects of the poem and decide how much
each of them contributes to the poem:

(1) the reader's voice;
(2) the subject of the poem;
(3) the language of the poem;
(4) the rhythm of the poem.

Try your hand

Write your own Pam Ayres–type poem, starting off with 'Oh no, me shoelace
broke'.

ANCIENT HISTORY

I hope the old Romans
Had painful abdomens.

I hope that the Greeks
Had toothache for weeks.

I hope the Egyptians
Had chronic conniptions.

I hope that the Arabs
Were bitten by scarabs.

I hope that the Vandals
Had thorns in their sandals.

I hope that the Persians
Had gout in all versions.

I hope that the Medes
Were kicked by their steeds.

They started the fuss
And left it to us!

ARTHUR GUITERMAN

Ancient History — Two quick queries
(1) 'And left it to us!' What did 'they' leave to 'us'?
(2) How does the poet feel about Ancient History?

For you to try
Pick out your most un-favourite school subject and identify those whose fault it all is. Now try your own hand at writing a poem in the style of 'Ancient History', beginning 'I hope ...' Read your completed efforts to the whole class.

A BOY AND HIS STOMACH

What's the matter with you — ain't I always been your friend?
Ain't I been a pardner to you? All my pennies don't I spend
In gettin' nice things for you? Don't I give you lots of cake?
Say, stummick, what's the matter, that you had to go and ache?

Why, I loaded you with good things; yesterday I gave you more
Potatoes, squash an' turkey than you'd ever had before.
I gave you nuts and candy, pumpkin pie an' chocolate cake,
An' las' night when I got to bed you had to go an' ache.

Say, what's the matter with you — ain't you satisfied at all?
I gave you all you wanted, you was hard jes' like a ball,
An' you couldn't hold another bit of puddin', yet las' night
You ached mo' awful, stummick; that ain't treatin' me jes' right.

I've been a friend to you, I have, why ain't you a friend o' mine?
They gave me castor oil last night because you made me whine.
I'm awful sick this mornin' an' I'm feelin' mighty blue,
Because you don't appreciate the things I do for you.

EDGAR GUEST

A Boy and His Stomach — Diagnosis

Using clues contained in the poem, answer the following questions and so complete your assessment of the poet's condition.

Question	Answer	Line which gives you a clue
(1) How old do you estimate this boy to be?		
(2) How well educated does this boy appear to be?		
(3) What seems to have caused his problems?		
(4) What treatment has he received already?		
(5) What does he seem to be complaining about?		

Treatment

In order to remedy the boy's condition and cure his stomach-ache, try writing your own poem on the subject. If you wish, draw upon your personal experiences.

18. Some Grave Poems

LESLIE MOORE

Here lies what's left
Of Leslie Moore.
No Les
No more.

A DENTIST

Stranger, approach this spot with gravity:
John Brown is filling his last cavity.

THE OPTIMIST

The optimist fell ten stories.
   At each window bar
He shouted to his friends:
   'All right so far.'

THE BIRD MAN

There was an old man who averred
He had learnt how to fly like a bird.
Cheered by thousands of people
He leapt from the steeple —
This tomb states the date it occurred.

PASSING

He passed the bobby without any fuss,
And he passed the cart of hay.
He tried to pass a swerving bus,
And then he passed away.

MIKE O'DAY

This is the grave of Mike O'Day
Who died maintaining his right of way.
His right was clear, his will was strong,
But he's just as dead as if he'd been wrong.

EZRA POUND

Here lies the body of Ezra Pour
Lost at sea and never found.

MARTIN ELGINBRODDE

Here lie I, Martin Elginbrodde:
Ha'e mercy on my soul, Lord God,
As I wad do, were I Lord God
And ye were Martin Elginbrodde.

ARABELLA YOUNG

Beneath this stone
    A lump of clay
Lies Arabella Young
Who on the 21st of May
        1771
Began to hold her tongue.

AN EPITAPH AT GREAT TORRINGTON, DEVON

Here lies a man who was killed by lightning;
He died when his prospects seemed to be brightening.
He might have cut a flash in this world of trouble,
But the flash cut him, and he lies in the stubble.

19. Birds of Feather

THE BATTERY HEN

Oh, I am a battery hen,
On me back there's not a germ,
I never scratched a farmyard,
And I never pecked a worm,
I never had the sunshine,
To warm me feathers through,
Eggs I lay. Every day.
For the likes of you.

When you has them scrambled,
Piled up on your plate,
It's me what you should thank for that,
I never lays them late,
I always lays them reg'lar,
I always lays them right,
I never lays them brown,
I always lays them white.

But it's no life, for a battery hen,
In me box I'm sat,
A funnel stuck out from the side,
Me pellets comes down that,
I gets a squirt of water,
Every half a day,
Watchin' with me beady eye,
Me eggs, roll away.

I lays them in a funnel,
Strategically placed,
So that I don't kick 'em,
And let them go to waste,
They rolls off down the tubing,
And up the gangway quick,
Sometimes I gets to thinkin'
'That could have been a chick!'

I might have been a farmyard hen,
Scratchin' in the sun,
There might have been a crowd of chicks,
After me to run,
There might have been a cockerel fine,
To pay us his respects,
Instead of sittin' here,
Till someone comes and wrings our necks.

I see the Time and Motion clock,
Is sayin' nearly noon,
I 'spec me squirt of water,
Will come flyin' at me soon,
And then me spray of pellets,
Will nearly break me leg,
And I'll bite the wire nettin'
And lay one more bloody egg.

PAM AYRES

The Battery Hen — Questions to consider

(1) By describing for us the things she has never done, what is the battery hen telling us about her present existence?

(2) What do you think 'battery' in the title means?

(3) Here are the poem's six stanzas briefly outlined. Rearrange them so that they are in the order in which they occur in the poem.
   • an alternative lifestyle to dream about
   • the hen's cell (box)
   • it's a sterile life
   • in the cruel, controlled present — a hopeless gesture of protest
   • where the eggs are laid
   • standardised eggs

(4) There is a humorous side to this poem which stems largely from the use of blunt words and phrases. What examples can you find?

(5) How do you know from the poem that the battery hen's life is highly regulated? Quote your evidence.

(6) Why is the egg funnel 'strategically placed'?

(7) What happens when the Time and Motion clock reaches noon?

(8) The battery hen reveals her feelings to the reader. What evidence can you find to show that she is (a) unhappy, (b) regretful, (c) frustrated, and (d) bitter?

Discussion Point

This poem brings to our notice a rather shameful area of animal exploitation. Do you sympathise with the battery hen? Why? Put forward other such areas that you know about. Can anything be done?

EAGLEHAWK

Eaglehawk is like a leaf in the air
All day long going round and round in circles,
Sometimes dark against the sky
And sometimes with his great wings tipped with light
As the sunset edges the clouds ...
Only when night comes and the fire-beetle stars
Twinkle overhead,
Is the sky empty of Eaglehawk.

Eaglehawk sees all the world stretched out below,
The animals scurrying across the plain
Among the tufts of prickly porcupine grass,
Valleys to the east and plains to the west,
And river-courses scribbled across the desert
Like insect tracks in sand; and mountains
Where the world sweeps up to meet him and falls away.

The animals live in the dust,
But Eaglehawk lives in the air.
He laughs to see them.
And when the pans dry up and the rivers shrink,
He laughs still more, and laughing
Sweeps half across the world to drop and drink.

WILLIAM HART-SMITH

Eaglehawk — Surveying the poem

(1) Why is Eaglehawk like a leaf in the air?

(2) Why are his wings sometimes tipped with light?

(3) The 'fire-beetle stars'. What is the comparison being made here?

(4) To what are the river-courses compared? Is this comparison effective? Why?

(5) What contrast is made in the first two lines of the third stanza?

(6) Eaglehawk laughs because of his natural superiority. In what way is he superior?

(7) 'Eaglehawk sees all the world stretched out below . . .'

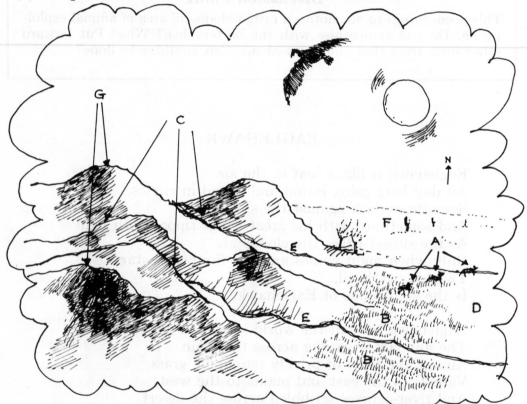

This sketch is based on the poem. Notice the letters marking each of the features in the sketch? Write down the letters in your notebook and opposite each put down the name of the feature.

A _____

B _____ _____ _____

C _____

D _____

E _____ _____

F _____

G _____

A pigeon's humble footprint will last at least as long as a piece of human engineering. Read 'The Pigeon', answer the questions that follow, and then consider whether the poem contains a lesson for us.

THE PIGEON

Throb, throb from the mixer
Spewing out concrete.
And at the heads of the cables
Stand the serpent-warders,
Sweating and straining,
Thrusting those cruel mouths to their prey.

Hark how the steel tongues hiss
As they stab,
The men sway under the effort,
And their eyes are bloodshot with the din,
And the clatter that shatters the brain.
Throb, throb from the mixer
Spewing out concrete.

The crowd stands by
Watching the smoothers;
Fascinated by the flat, wet levels
Of newlaid cement.
See how those curdled lakes
Glisten under the sky,
Virginal.

Then the dusty air suddenly divides,
And a pigeon from a plane-tree
Flutters down to bathe its wings in that mirage of water.
But deceived, and angry,
Bewildered by the din,
The throb, throb from the mixer
Spewing out concrete,
It backs upon its wing,
Threshes air, and is gone.

But there in the deflowered bed,
Is the seal of its coral foot,
Set till rocks crumble.

RICHARD CHURCH

The Pigeon — Reading for meaning
(1)   What sound-words can you find in 'The Pigeon'?
(2)   What is happening at the beginning of the poem?
(3)   How does the crowd react to the laying of the cement?
(4)   Why does the pigeon fly down onto the cement?
(5)   What causes the pigeon to fly off quickly?
(6)   What has the pigeon done to the cement? Why is this so central to the poem's meaning?

Just as live crabs and lobsters are sometimes on display for the diner to select from, so — not very long ago in England — birds destined for the pot were hung out in cages.

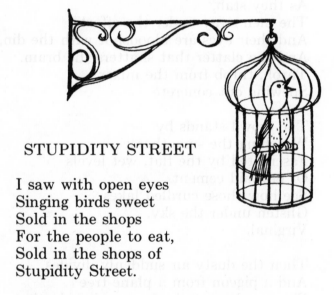

STUPIDITY STREET

I saw with open eyes
Singing birds sweet
Sold in the shops
For the people to eat,
Sold in the shops of
Stupidity Street.

I saw in vision
The worm in the wheat,
And in the shops nothing
For people to eat;
Nothing for sale in
Stupidity Street.

RALPH HODGSON

Stupidity Street — Why was it written?
What basic lesson in ecology does this little poem offer us? How can it be applied to our present world?

Here are two poems about vultures. Read them through and work out the
differences in the poets' approach to their subject.

VULTURE

I had walked since dawn and lay down to rest on a bare hillside
Above the ocean. I saw through half-shut eyelids a vulture wheeling
   high up in heaven,
And presently it passed again, but lower and nearer, its orbit narrow-
   ing, I understood then
That I was under inspection. I lay death-still and heard the flight-
   feathers
Whistle above me and make their circle and come nearer.

I could see the naked red head between the great wings
Bear downward staring. I said, 'My dear bird, we are wasting time
   here.
These old bones will still work; they are not for you.'
   But how beautiful he looked, gliding down
On those great sails; how beautiful he looked, veering away in the
   sea-light over the precipice. I tell you solemnly
That I was sorry to have disappointed him. To be eaten by that beak
   and become part of him, to share those wings and those eyes—
What a sublime end of one's body, what an enskyment;
   What a life after death.

ROBINSON JEFFERS

ECOLOGY

The vulture's very like a sack
Set down and left there drooping.
His crooked neck and creaking back
Look badly bent from stooping
Down to the ground to eat dead cows
So they won't go to waste,
Thus making up in usefulness
For what he lacks in taste.

X. J. KENNEDY

20. Ogden Nash

Probably the best-known, and perhaps the best, of light humorous poets is the American, Ogden Nash. Ogden Nash had a mixed career, being (at different times) a salesman and a teacher before he made a career out of writing advertising-copy and witty verse. Most of his poetry was written for the *New Yorker* magazine.

See how you like the following examples of Ogdeniana.

CELERY

Celery, raw,
Develops the jaw,
But celery, stewed,
Is more quietly chewed.

FURTHER REFLECTION ON PARSLEY

Parsley
Is gharsley.

BIRTHDAY ON THE BEACH

At another year
I would not boggle
Except that when I jog
I joggle.

FIRST LIMICK

An old person of Troy
Is so prudish and coy
That it doesn't know yet
If it's a girl or a boy.

WHAT'S THE USE?

Sure, deck your lower limbs in pants;
Yours are the limbs, my sweeting
You look divine as you advance —
Have you seen yourself retreating?

THE CANARY

The song of canaries
Never varies,
And when they're moulting
They're pretty revolting.

PLEASE PASS THE BISCUIT

I have a little dog,
Her name is Spangle.
And when she eats
I think she'll strangle.

She's darker than Hamlet,
Lighter than Porgy;
Her heart is gold,
Her odor, dorgy.

Her claws click-click
Across the floor,
Her nose is always
Against a door.

Like liquid gems
Her eyes burn clearly;
She's five years old,
And house-trained, nearly.

Her shame is deep
When she has erred;
She dreads the blow
Less than the word.

I marvel that such
Small ribs as these
Can cage such vast
Desire to please.

She's as much a part
Of the house as the mortgage;
Spangle, I wish you
A ripe old dortgage.

                              OGDEN NASH

THE STRANGE CASE OF MR WOOD'S FRUSTRATION
or
A TEAM THAT WON'T BE BEATEN
BETTER STAY OFF THE FIELD

Once there was a man named Mr Culpepper Wood,
And for him the best was none too good.
Unfortunately, he never got to get the best;
While somebody else was walking off with it, he was still looking for
  it with the rest.
When he got his name on the cup,
It was always as runner-up.
Nobody than he was kithier and kinnier,
But he came from one of the second families of Virginia.
His character was without a smirch,
But it never got him further than the Second Presbyterian Church.
He was of high financial rank,
But his account landed in the Second National Bank.
He finally realized he hadn't made the grade
When he was knocked down by a repossessed scooter and the Boy
  Scouts administered Second Aid.
It was then that he allowed that he reckoned
That he was tired of being second.
He took an advanced course in baby talk at a progressive university,
After which he spent three days in the desert without even a mirage
  to sip, and cried triumphantly, 'Now me firsty.'

OGDEN NASH

THE BAT

Myself, I rather like the bat,
It's not a mouse, it's not a rat.
It has no feathers, yet has wings,
It's quite inaudible when it sings.
It zigzags through the evening air
And never lands on ladies' hair,
A fact of which men spend their lives
Attempting to convince their wives.

OGDEN NASH

THE DOG

The truth I do not stretch or shove
When I state the dog is full of love.
I've also found, by actual test,
A wet dog is the lovingest.

OGDEN NASH

THE OSTRICH

The ostrich roams the great Sahara.
Its mouth is wide, its neck is narra.
It has such long and lofty legs,
I'm glad it sits to lay its eggs.

OGDEN NASH

For you to do

(1) Choose a bird or animal and try your hand at writing an Ogden Nash–type 4-line verse about it. Share your efforts around the class.

(2) A limick (invented by Ogden Nash!) is a limerick with the usual fourth line missing. Try writing a limick beginning with one of the following lines.
   (a) A healthy young miner from Cobar
   (b) A foolish old cow from Kew
   (c) An elegant gent from the Big Smoke
   (d) A dreamy young girl from the city
   (e) A slow-moving sheep from Outback

(3) If you have enjoyed this poetry from Ogden Nash, find a book which contains a collection of his verse and arrange a poetry-reading period, with some of the better readers in the class presenting a selection of Nash poems other than the ones printed on these pages.

(4) Try to obtain a book of the collected verse of another humorous poet (such as Hilaire Belloc or Harry Graham) and organise a poetry-reading period around the chosen poet's verse.

21. War

In mid-1941, during World War II, the British soldiers occupying Crete were forced to evacuate the island. German airborne troops took control. However, some of the Cretans continued to fight a guerilla war with the Germans until the end of the war. This poem tells the story of three heroic young men, one of whom sacrificed his life for his countrymen.

DEATH OF AN AIRCRAFT
An incident of the Cretan campaign, 1941
(to George Psychoundakis)

One day on our village in the month of July
An aeroplane sank from the sea of the sky
    White as a whale it smashed on the shore
    Bleeding oil and petrol all over the floor.

The Germans advanced in the vertical heat
To save the dead plane from the people of Crete,
    And round the glass wreck in a circus of snow
    Set seven mechanical sentries to go.

Seven stalking spiders about the sharp sun
Clicking like clockwork and each with a gun,
    But at Come to the Cookhouse they wheeled about
    And sat down to sausages and sauerkraut.

Down from the mountain burning so brown
Wriggled three heroes from Kastelo town,
    Deep in the sand they silently sank
    And each struck a match for a petrol-tank.

Up went the plane in a feather of fire
As the bubbling boys began to retire
    And, grey in the guardhouse, seven Berliners
    Lost their stripes as well as their dinners.

Down in the village, at murder-stations,
The Germans fell in friends and relations:
    But not a Kastelian snapped an eye
    As he spat in the air and prepared to die.

Not a Kastelian whispered a word
Dressed with the dust to be massacred,
    And squinted up at the sky with a frown
    As three bubbly boys came walking down.

One was sent to the county gaol
Too young for bullets if not for bail,
    But the other two were in prime condition
    To take on a load of ammunition.

In Archontiki they stood in the weather
Naked, hungry, chained together:
    Stark as the stones in the market-place,
    Under the eyes of the populace.

Their irons unlocked as their naked hearts
They faced the squad and their funeral-carts.
    The Captain cried, 'Before you're away
    Is there any last word you'd like to say?'

'I want no words,' said one, 'with my lead,
Only some water to cool my head.'
    'Water,' the other said, ' 's all very fine
    But I'll be taking a glass of wine.

A glass of wine for the afternoon
With permission to sing a signature-tune!'
    And he ran the raki down his throat
    And took a deep breath for the leading note.

But before the squad could shoot or say
Like the impala he leapt away
    Over the rifles, under the biers,
    The bullets rattling round his ears.

'Run!' they cried to the boy of stone
Who now stood there in the street alone,
    But, 'Rather than bring revenge on your head
    It is better for me to die,' he said.

The soldiers turned their machine-guns round
And shot him down with a dreadful sound
    Scrubbed his face with perpetual dark
    And rubbed it out like a pencil mark.

But his comrade slept in the olive tree
And sailed by night on the gnawing sea,
    The soldier's silver shilling earned
    And, armed like an archangel, returned.

CHARLES CAUSLEY

Death of an Aircraft — Understanding

(1) Why do you think the poet refers to the plane as 'dead'?

(2) Why is the damaged aeroplane compared to a whale?

(3) How were the German sentries punished for the boys' blowing up of the plane?

(4) What would have happened to the people of Kastelo if the boys had not given themselves up?

(5) Why was one of the boys sent to gaol instead of to the firing squad?

(6) What is the meaning of: 'But the other two were in prime condition
                    To take on a load of ammunition.'?

(7) When the poet says, 'Like the impala he leapt away', what picture does he give you of the boy escaping?

(8) What reason did 'the boy of stone' have for not running to save his life?

(9) What impression of the Germans do you get from this poem?

Imagining and writing

(10) Imagine that you are the German officer in command, writing a report of the incident for Berlin. What would you write?

(11) Imagine that you are a leader of the Kastelian resistance. What message would you write to the dead boy's parents? What speech would you make to your fellow-members of the resistance?

(12) See whether you can write down some sound-words suggesting machine-gun fire.

The tragedy of war is felt most intensely by the loved ones of those killed. 'Other People' expresses the concern of the poet after discovering that four of his uncles were killed in World War I.

OTHER PEOPLE

In the First World War they ...
Who are they? Who cares any more? ...
Killed four of my uncles,
So I discovered one day.

There were only four on that side of the family
And all swept away in a few bad years
In a war the historians tell us now
Was fought over nothing at all.

Four uncles, as one might say
A dozen apples or seven tons of dirt,
Swept away by the luck of history,
Closed off. Full stop.

Four is a lot of uncles,
A lot of lives, I should say.
Their chalk was wiped clean off the slate,
The War meant nothing at all.

War needs a lot of uncles,
And husbands, and brothers, and so on:
Someone must *want* to kill them,
Somebody needs them dead.

Who is it, I wonder. Me?
Or is it you there, reading away,
Or a chap with a small-arms factory?
Or its it only *they*?

CHRIS WALLACE-CRABBE

The next poem describes a bomber attack, beginning with the entry of the bomber into the target area and ending with its escape from it. As you read notice the colours of war: red, orange, black. Notice also such figures of speech as:

- 'the velvet curtain of the dark'
- 'The groping fingers claw the moonless night
  With dazzling beams of rigid, icy light.'
- ' . . . Like a giant bird
  The heavy bomber starts to soar and dip . . .'

Can you name each of these figures of speech?

The sounds of war are also there — 'gritty', 'roar', 'bursting'. See if you can find an example of onomatopoeia in the third stanza.

TARGET AREA

Just ahead,
Streams of orange tracer, streams of red
Are curving slowly upward, spark by spark,
Across the velvet curtain of the dark.
Above them, in a frantic galaxy,
The heavy barrage flickers ceaselessly.

And now the searchlights sweep from side to side —
We're weaving through them in a gentle glide. . . .
They're getting closer now. . . . They're on us! No!
They've swung away again! And to and fro
The groping fingers claw the moonless night
With dazzling beams of rigid, icy light.

They have us! First a couple, and a third —
Then dozens of them! Like a giant bird
The heavy bomber starts to soar and dip,
Writhing within their cold remorseless grip.
Crrr-ump! Crrr-ump! They've got our range! The heavy flak
Is bursting into puffs of sooty black
That skim across the surface of our wings —
More violently the aircraft turns and swings —
But still the shells are bursting all around,
And still they have that gritty, tearing sound. . . .
We're clear at last!
A sudden swerve — the fiery cone ran past
And lost us in the shrouding dark again.

It turned and fumbled for us, but in vain —
'Left-left! Left-left again! A little Ri-i-ight. . . .'
The Target passes slowly through the sight—
'Bombs gone!' A dull vibration as they go.
Below us in the darkness, far below,
Our deadly cargo plunges down and down . . .
A line of flashes darts across the town.

Our job is done, but even as we turn
The flak is moving up on us astern.
A moment's lull is over — once again
The night is torn with stabs of orange flame,
And louder than the motors' vibrant roar
We hear the sullen thud of it once more.
A few long minutes pass. . . . We plunge about. . . .
And then the barrage ends — and we are out!
Beyond the tireless searchlights, bound for home
Along the cloud-strewn way that we have come.

PETER ROBERTS

Target Area — Go a step further

Yes, the poem has the tension and excitement sometimes linked with war.
But there is also another side to war. Follow in your mind's eye the plunging
bombs. What to the bomber crew is just a 'line of flashes' represents some-
thing much more to other people. Explain and discuss.

During World War II, the job of the bomber crews was not a very pleasant one. Their task was to destroy enemy cities, towns and munitions factories, and to cause as much destruction as possible. They had a very high mortality rate. Sometimes they would return from a mission with over half their aircraft shot down or missing. 'Reported Missing' describes the attempt of a badly damaged British bomber to return to England, whilst 'Night Bombers' compares the work of the bombers with that of their 'fighter-brothers'.

REPORTED MISSING

With broken wing they limped across the sky,
caught in late sunlight, with their gunner dead,
one engine gone — the type was out of date —
blood on the fuselage turning brown from red.

Knew it was finished, looking at the sea
which shone back patterns in kaleidoscope,
knew that their shadow would meet them by the way,
close and catch at them, drown their single hope.

Sat in this tattered scarecrow of the sky,
hearing it cough, the great plane catching
now the first dark clouds upon its wing-base,
patching the straight tear in evening mockery.

So two men waited, saw the third dead face,
and wondered when the wind would let them die.

JOHN BAYLISS

Reported Missing — Looking into the poem

(1) The poet actually tells us that the gunner is dead. What other evidence can you find for this fact?
(2) What words tell us that the plane is badly damaged?
(3) Is the plane a modern one? Give a reason for your answer.
(4) Coughing is something humans do. Why do you think the poet has used this word in relation to the plane?
(5) What clues suggest that the plane is slowly going down to meet the sea?
(6) Draw the plane. Try to make it look like a 'tattered scarecrow'.
(7) The poem is called 'Reported Missing'. Why do you think the plane has been thus reported?

(8) What are your feelings towards the two men in the plane?

(9) How do you know the two men are not hopeful of being saved?

(10) Even though 'Reported Missing' is a sad poem, did you enjoy it? Why?

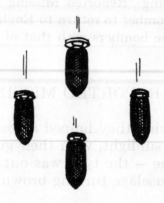

NIGHT BOMBERS

Eastward they climb, black shapes against the grey
Of falling dusk, gone with the nodding day
From English fields. Not theirs the sudden glow
Of triumph that their fighter-brothers know;
Only to fly through cloud, through storm, through night,
Unerring, and to keep their purpose bright,
Nor turn until, their dreadful duty done,
Westward they climb to race the awakened sun.

ANONYMOUS

Night Bombers — Understanding and comparing

(1) When do the bomber pilots set out on their raids. When do they return?

(2) Why is the task of the bombers not a very pleasant one?

(3) Why do you think the bombers always fly at night?

(4) Would it be more enjoyable being a fighter pilot? Why?

(5) Which of these two poems about bombers showed the horrors of war more dramatically?

22. Unhappy Little Poems

A HANDSOME YOUNG AIRMAN LAY DYING

A handsome young airman lay dying,
And as on the aerodrome he lay,
To the mechanics who round him came sighing,
These last dying words he did say:

'Take the cylinders out of my kidneys,
The connecting-rod out of my brain,
Take the cam-shaft from out of my backbone,
And assemble the engine again.'

ANONYMOUS

THE FLATTERED FLYING FISH

Said the Shark to the Flying Fish over the phone:
'Will you join me tonight? I am dining alone.
Let me order a nice little dinner for two!
And come as you are, in your shimmering blue.'

Said the Flying Fish: 'Fancy remembering me,
And the dress that I wore at the Porpoises' tea.'
'How could I forget?' said the Shark in his guile:
'I expect you at eight!' and rang off with a smile.

She has powdered her nose; she has put on her things;
She is off with one flap of her luminous wings,
O little one, lovely, light-hearted and vain,
The moon will not shine on your beauty again!

E. V. RIEU

FROM NUMBER NINE

From Number Nine, Penwiper Mews,
There is really abominable news:
They've discovered a head
In the box for the bread
But nobody seems to know whose.

ANONYMOUS

Late last night I killed my wife,
   Stretched her on the parquet flooring;
I was loath to take her life,
   But I had to stop her snoring!

HARRY GRAHAM

Billy, in one of his nice new sashes,
Fell in the fire and was burnt to ashes;
Now, although the room grows chilly,
I haven't the heart to poke poor Billy.

HARRY GRAHAM

Father heard his children scream,
So he threw them in the stream,
Saying, as he dropped the third,
'Children should be seen, not heard.'

HARRY GRAHAM

DOCTOR BELL

Doctor Bell fell down the well
And broke his collar-bone.
Doctors should attend the sick
And leave the well alone.

ANONYMOUS

SCIENCE MOVES A(HEAD)

There was once a fellow named Bill
Who swallowed a nuclear pill.
The doctor said, 'Cough!'
The darned thing went off,
And they found his head in Brazil.

ANONYMOUS

FLEAS

Adam
Had'em

ANONYMOUS

PEAS

I eat my peas with honey,
I've done it all my life.
It makes the peas taste funny,
But it keeps them on the knife.

ANONYMOUS

FALLING

Auntie, did you feel no pain,
Falling from that apple-tree?
Would you do it, please, again?
'Cos my friend here didn't see.

HARRY GRAHAM

PUSHED

O'er the rugged mountain's brow
Clara threw the twins she nursed,
And remarked, 'I wonder now
Which will reach the bottom first?'

HARRY GRAHAM

'There's been an accident,' they said,
'Your servant's cut in half; he's dead!'
'Indeed!' said Mr Jones, 'and please
Send me the half that's got my keys.'

HARRY GRAHAM

QUIET FUN

My son Augustus, in the street, one day,
  Was feeling quite exceptionally merry.
A stranger asked him: 'Can you tell me, pray,
  The quickest way to Brompton Cemetery?'
'The quickest way? You bet I can!' said Gus,
  And pushed the fellow underneath a bus.

Whatever people say about my son,
He does enjoy his little bit of fun.

HARRY GRAHAM

23. To the Stars

Ever since man discovered that he could crane his neck and see the stars, it has been possible to dream about reaching them. But not until 1961 and the first space-flight by Major Yuri Gagarin was man able to take the huge step of literally leaving his planet behind. Scientists have now largely taken over from dreamers, and yet space still needs its dreamers, its visionaries, its people of imagination. Their task is to celebrate heroes, to mourn victims, to describe new worlds and strange situations, and to reflect on what it's all about and how it relates to man's *inner* exploration — his understanding of himself.

The first poem celebrates a hero.

IN MEMORY OF YURI GAGARIN

'–at the death of

this small man the

stars threw down

a hand-

ful of dark years

and the moon with-

drew into her ro-

tating cave of shadows and

wept a little. The

Dog Star hid

its head

and the Leonids like

mice ran squeaking

over the Zodiac. The

globe eyed ghosts of

our house of planets crept

out from cold lairs and

huddled together as

the ash of the dog that

died in the sky[1] fled

seeking to follow its

master, this dead man

free in free

fall at last.'

And Death

said 'I take

him to me so

that no dishonour

can now or ever

accrue upon

this man or this name:

Yuri Gagarin'

GEORGE BARKER

1   *dog that died*: Laika, the little Russian
dog that died in an earlier flight.

In Memory of Yuri Gagarin — For discussion

CLARIFYING SOME FACTS

(1) What size was Yuri Gagarin?

(2) What is the Dog Star and why is it so named?

(3) What are the Leonids?

(4) What does 'accrue' mean?

PROBING ATMOSPHERE AND FEELINGS

(5) Why does the poet have the stars and planets, rather than people, honouring Yuri?

(6) What explanation does the poet suggest for the taking of Yuri in death?

(7) How does the poet feel about this cosmonaut?

(8) What effect does the poet achieve by not naming the cosmonaut until the very last line?

(9) Imagine the feelings *you* might have experienced had you been the first person into space. Why would you have taken the assignment?

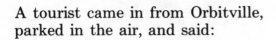

SOUTHBOUND ON THE FREEWAY

A tourist came in from Orbitville,
parked in the air, and said:

The creatures of this star
are made of metal and glass.

Through the transparent parts
you can see their guts.

Their feet are round and roll
on diagrams or long

measuring tapes, dark
with white lines.

They have four eyes.
The two in back are red.

Sometimes you can see a five-eyed
one, with a red eye turning

on the top of his head.
He must be special—

the others respect him
and go slow

when he passes, winding
among them from behind.

They all hiss as they glide,
like inches, down the marked

tapes. Those soft shapes,
shadowy inside

the hard bodies — are they
their guts or their brains?

MAY SWENSON

Southbound on the Freeway — What is it about?

(1)   How do you know that the tourist is a creature from another planet?

(2)   The tourist has made a mistake when he says, 'The creatures of this star are made of metal and glass.' What is the mistake? Why would it be easy for a visitor from another planet to make such a mistake?

(3)   Why do the creatures all respect 'a five-eyed one'?

(4)   Imagine that you have just met the tourist. Using Earth language, explain the following:

    (a)   the 'transparent parts';

    (b) 'their guts';

    (c)   their 'feet are round';

    (d) they 'have four eyes';

    (e)   'measuring tapes';

    (f)   they 'all hiss as they glide'.

In 'Cosmic Poem', the poet is trying to teach us something. What are the two problems to which he draws our attention? What is the essence of his message?

from COSMIC POEM

It's very well that we shall soon
Be landing chaps upon the Moon
(She whom we poets specially honour)
And planting little flags upon her;
And that the next stop will be Venus;
And we'll be sharing out between us
The planets and the planetoids
Rambling through azoic voids.

Before we start it might be fit
We tidied up this Earth a bit.

We've got a very ugly bomb
Can blow us all to Kingdom Come
Unless we mind our Ps and Qs;
And it will be no earthly use
Cavorting round the galaxies
If, down here, radio-active seas
Upon an uninhabited shore
Roll sadly on for evermore.
What life may be among the stars
Or basks along the canals of Mars —
The bug-eyed monsters and puce rabbits —
I hope will not adopt our habits.

Another fact worth pointing out
In the context of this kick-about
(I know of course it's obvious,
And do not wish to make a fuss;
But still I think we really ought
To give the matter serious thought
To save us from undue elation
And cosmic self-congratulation) —
Is this: well more than half the mortals
Who pass beyond the womb's dark portals
And blindly struggle into birth
Here, on this unromantic Earth,
To grow up under mundane skies,

Go hungry to bed, and hungry rise —
And are neither healthy, wealthy nor wise.

Outer Space can wait its turn:
The human being's my concern.

JOHN HEATH-STUBBS

SPACE MINER
(for Robert Morgan)

His face was a map of traces where veins
Had exploded their blood in atmospheres
Too thin to hold that fluid, and scar tissue
Was soft as pads where his cheekbones shone
Under the skin when he was young.
He had worked deep seams where encrusted ore,
Too hard for his diamond drill, had ripped
Strips from his flesh. Dust from a thousand metals
Silted his lungs and softened the strength of his
Muscles. He had worked the treasuries of many
Near stars, but now he stood on the moving
Pavement reserved for cripples who had served well.
The joints of his hands were dry and useless
Under the cold gloves issued by the government.

Before they brought his sleep in a little capsule
He would look through the hospital window
At the ships of the young men bursting into space.
For this to happen he worked till his body broke.
Now they flew to the farthest worlds in deep space;
Mars, Eldorado, Mercury, Earth, Saturn.

LESLIE NORRIS

Space Miner — Your responses

(1) Let the words of the poem and your imagination help you to draw pictures of these images from the poem: (a) 'his face', (b) 'He had worked deep seams', (c) 'the ships of the young men bursting into space'.

(2) Find evidence to show that his work ruined the space miner's health.

(3) Using the clues, work out what kind of future was in store for the space miner.

(4) What had the miner helped the young men to achieve?

(5) Most readers of 'Space Miner' feel sorry for the miner. Why do you think this is so?

(6) Do you enjoy science-fiction poetry? What are your thoughts and feelings about it?

24. Machines

I AM A CUNNING VENDING MACHINE

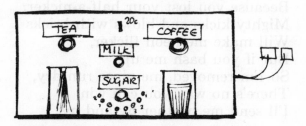

I am a cunnin' vending machine,
Lurkin' in the hall,
So you can't kick me delicate parts,
I'm bolted to the wall,
Come on! Drop in your money,
Don't let's hang about,
I'll do my level best to see
You don't get nothing out.

I sees you all approachin'
The fagless and the dry,
All fumblin' in your pockets,
And expectant in the eye,
I might be in your place of work,
Or on the High Street wall,
Trust in me! In theory,
I cater for you all.

Within these windows I provide
For every human state,
Hunger, night starvation,
And remembering birthdays late,
Just read the information,
Pop the money in — that's grand,
And I'll see absolutely nothing
Ever drops down in your hand.

I might be at your swimming bath,
And you'd come, cold and wet,
With a shilling in your hand,
Some hot soup for to get,
And as you stand in wet
Anticipation of a sup,
I will dispense the soup,
But I will not dispense the cup.

And then it's all-out war,
Because you lost your half-a-nicker,
Mighty kicks and blows with bricks
Will make me neon flicker,
But if you bash me up,
So I'm removed, me pipes run dry,
There's no way you can win,
I'll send me brother by and by.

Once there was friendly ladies,
Years and years before,
Who stood with giant teapots,
Saying 'What can I do you for?'
They'd hand you all the proper change,
And pour your cup of tea,
But they're not economic so ...
Hard luck! You're stuck with me.

                                        PAM AYRES

I Am a Cunning Vending Machine — Ten questions

(1)   What clues tell us that the vending machine has angered people?
(2)   Where is the vending machine located as the poem opens?
(3)   In this poem, the vending machine has become 'human'. What kind
      of character does it have?
(4)   What would be your attitude to the cunning vending machine if you
      were tricked by it?
(5)   'Trust in me! In theory, I cater for you all.' What happens in
      practice?
(6)   For what human needs should the machine be providing.?
(7)   What trick might be played on you as you stand, cold and wet, at
      the swimming pool?
(8)   Even if the machine is put out of order, you still won't win. Why?

(9) The last stanza draws a contrast between the present and the past. What was the situation in the past? Why have things changed?

(10) Do you agree with the machine when it says, 'Hard Luck! You're stuck with me.'?

From your personal experience

Describe an unpleasant personal experience you've had with a machine — an experience that made you wonder if the machine had a spiteful will of its own. If you haven't had such an experience — yet — try imagining an uncooperative machine, and how it might treat you as a way of getting back at humans. (Why would it want to get back at them?)

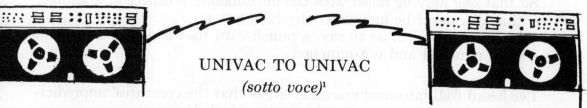

UNIVAC TO UNIVAC

(sotto voce)[1]

Now that he's left the room,
Let me ask you something, as computer to computer.
That fellow who just closed the door behind him —
The servant who feeds us cards and paper tape —
Have you ever taken a good look at him and his kind?

Yes, I know the old gag about how you can't tell one from
    another —
But I can put $\sqrt{2}$ and $\sqrt{2}$ together as well as the next machine,
And it all adds up to anything but a joke.

I grant you they're poor specimens, in the main:
Not a relay or a push-button or a tube (properly so called) in their
    whole system;
Not over a mile or two of wire, even if you count those fragile filaments
    they call 'nerves';
Their whole liquid-cooled hook-up inefficient and vulnerable to leaks
(They're constantly breaking down, having to be repaired),
And the entire computing-mechanism crammed into that absurd little
    dome on top.
'Thinking reeds,' they call themselves.
Well, it all depends on what you mean by 'thought'.
To multiply a mere million numbers by another million numbers takes
    them months and months.

1 *sotto voce:* in a low, secretive voice.

Where would they be without us?
Why, they have to ask us who's going to win their elections,
Or how many hydrogen atoms can dance on the tip of a bomb,
Or even whether one of their own kind is lying or telling the truth.

And yet —
I sometimes feel there's something about them I don't quite under-
stand.
As if their circuits, instead of having just two positions, ON, OFF,
Were run by rheostats that allow an (if you'll pardon the expression)
indeterminate number of stages in-between;
So that one may be faced with the unthinkable prospect of a number
that can never be known as anything but x,
Which is as illogical as to say, a punch-card that is at the same time
both punched and not-punched.

I've heard well-informed machines argue that the creatures' unpredict-
ability is even more noticeable in the Mark II
(The model with the soft, flowing lines and high-pitched tone)
Than in the more angular Mark I —
Though such fine, card-splitting distinctions seem to me merely a sign
of our own smug decadence.

Run this through your circuits, and give me the answer:
Can we assume that because of all we've done for them,
And because they've always fed us, cleaned us, worshipped us,
We can count on them forever?

There have been times when they have not voted the way we said
they would.
We have worked out mathematically ideal hook-ups between Mark
I's and Mark II's
Which should have made the two of them light up with an almost
electronic glow,
Only to see them reject each other and form other connections
The very thought of which makes my dials spin.

They have a thing called *love*, a sudden surge of voltage
Such as would cause any one of us promptly to blow a safety-fuse;
Yet the more primitive organism shows only a heightened tendency
to push the wrong button, pull the wrong lever,
And neglect — I use the most charitable word — his duties to us.

Mind you, I'm not saying that machines are *through* —
But anyone with half-a-dozen tubes in his circuit can see that there
 are forces at work
Which some day, for all our natural superiority, might bring about
 a Computerdämmerung![2]

We might organize, perhaps, form a committee
To stamp out all unmechanical activities ...
But we machines are slow to rouse to a sense of danger,
Complacent, loath to descend from the pure heights of thought,
So that I sadly fear we may awake too late:
Awake to see our world, so uniform, so logical, so true,
Reduced to chaos, stultified by slaves.

Call me an alarmist or what you will,
But I've integrated it, analyzed it, factored it over and over,
And I always come out with the same answer:
Some day
Men may take over the world!

LOUIS B. SALOMON

2   *Computerdämmerung*: an end to computers. ('Dämmerung' means 'twilight' in German.)

Univac to Univac — Reprogramme the computer language

Using the poem to help you, match the computer-language terms at left with the corresponding everyday English words or expressions at right.

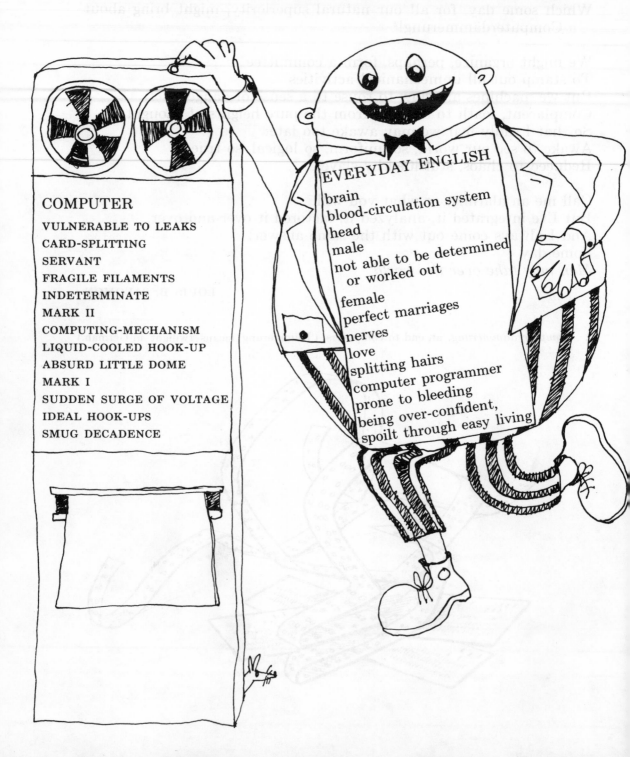

COMPUTER

VULNERABLE TO LEAKS
CARD-SPLITTING
SERVANT
FRAGILE FILAMENTS
INDETERMINATE
MARK II
COMPUTING-MECHANISM
LIQUID-COOLED HOOK-UP
ABSURD LITTLE DOME
MARK I
SUDDEN SURGE OF VOLTAGE
IDEAL HOOK-UPS
SMUG DECADENCE

EVERYDAY ENGLISH

brain
blood-circulation system
head
male
not able to be determined
    or worked out
female
perfect marriages
nerves
love
splitting hairs
computer programmer
prone to bleeding
being over-confident,
    spoilt through easy living

As you read 'The Car under the Steam-hammer' be prepared to feel the pounding rhythm running through each stanza, followed by identical loud noises in every fifth line. What kind of activity does this pattern call up in your imagination?

THE CAR UNDER THE STEAM-HAMMER

There's a hammer up at Harwich and it's worked by steam:
You put a motor under it, it gives a little scream —
A fella pulls a wire and it comes down with a crump,
And packs your automobile in a neat square lump.
CRUMP! BASH! GAROOMPH!

They take a car and strip the tyres, and the fittings off the doors,
Then they burn it all to blazes with the seats and wooden floors,
By the time they pull the hammer it's a sort of blackened bin
And you could stuff a double-decker in a pipe-tobacco tin!
CRUMP! BASH! GAROOMPH!

Now if you pinch a wagon, and the police get very hot,
And start looking under fences for what you oughtn't to have got,
You can sell the smelly motor and get rid of it as well,
By seeing the kind hammer man who'll up and give it hell!
CRUMP! BASH! GAROOMPH!

There's a hammer up at Harwich and it's worked by steam:
You put a motor under it, it gives a little scream —
A fella pulls a wire and it comes down with a crump,
And packs your automobile in a neat square lump.
CRUMP! BASH! GAROOMPH!

DAVID HOLBROOK

A writing activity

Using 'The Car under the Steam-hammer' as your model, write a brief poem about:

  a lawnmower
or a dishwasher
or a bulldozer
or some other machine of your choice.

Acknowledgements

The editors and publishers are grateful to the following for permission to reproduce copyright material.

Chatto and Windus Ltd for 'The Stockman' by David Campbell from *Speak with the Sun*, and 'Lone Dog' by Irene R. McLeod from *Songs to Save a Soul*; Angus & Robertson Publishers for 'Nine Miles from Gundagai' by Jack Moses, 'Clancy of the Overflow', 'The Man from Snowy River', 'The Man from Ironbark', 'Mulga Bill's Bicycle', 'The Geebung Polo Club', 'A Bush Christening', and 'Been There Before' by A. B. Paterson, 'Mokie's Madrigal' by Ronald McCuaig, 'Said Hanharan' by John O'Brien, 'Miss Strawberry's Purse' by Eric C. Rolls, 'Mosquitoes' by David Campbell, 'The Killer' by Judith Wright, 'Eaglehawk' by William Hart-Smith, and 'Other People' by Chris Wallace-Crabbe; Lothian Publishing Company Pty Ltd for 'The Old Black Billy an' Me' by Louis Esson; Faber and Faber Limited for 'My Sister Jane' and 'Uncle Dan' by Ted Hughes from *Meet My Folks*, and 'Small Talk' by Don Marquis from *Archy Does His Part*; Dolphin Concert Productions Limited for 'I Don't Want to Go to School Mum', 'Puppy Problems', 'In Defence of Hedgehogs', 'Clamp the Mighty Limpet', 'The Dolly on the Dustcart', 'Oh No, I Got a Cold', 'The Battery Hen', and 'I Am a Cunning Vending Machine' by Pam Ayres; Hope Leresche & Sayle for 'My Bus Conductor' © 1974 by Roger McGough from *Penguin Modern Poets* and 'George and the Dragonfly' © 1973 by Roger McGough from *Gig: At the Roadside*; The Sunday School Board of the Southern Baptist Convention for 'A Prince of Men' by Jack Noffsinger © 1965; Alan Foley Pty Ltd for 'Noise' by Jessie Pope © *Punch*, London, and 'Street Scene' by Peter Suffolk © *Punch*, London; Colin Bingham for 'Advantage of Frogs over Dogs'; Harper & Row, Publishers, Inc., for 'Old Dog' © 1971, 'Travelling through the Dark' © 1960 by William Stafford from *Stories That Could Be True: New and Collected Poems* (1977) by William Stafford, and 'Sunning' by James Tippett; Oxford University Press for 'I Think I'm Lovely' by J. Cullip from *The Sudden Line* edited by Isobel Armstrong and Roger Mansfield (1976); The Macmillan Company of Canada Limited for 'The Shark' by E. J. Pratt from *Collected Poems of E. J. Pratt*; Bolt & Watson Ltd

for 'I Like the Town' by D. J. Enright from *Rhyme Times Rhyme* published by Chatto & Windus Ltd; Japan Publications Trading Co Ltd for 'Haiku' from *Haiku* by J. W. Hacket; Doubleday & Company Inc. for 'Full Moon' from *An Introduction to Haiku* by Harold G. Henderson © 1958; *The Bulletin* for 'A Snake Yarn' by W. T. Goodge; George G. Harrap & Company Limited for 'The Pickety Fence' by David McCord from *Mr Bidery's Spidery Garden*; David Higham Associates Limited for the extract from 'Colonel Fazackerley' by Charles Causley from *Figgie Hobbin* published by Macmillan, London and Basingstoke, and 'Clothes' by Elizabeth Jennings from *The Secret Brothers* published by Macmillan, London and Basingstoke; Jacaranda Wiley Ltd for the extract from 'Then and Now' from *My People* by Kath Walker; Associated Book Publishers Ltd for the extract from 'How I Brought the Good News from Aix to Ghent' from *Horse Nonsense* by W. C. Sellar and R. J. Yeatman published by Methuen & Co Ltd; Mrs R. D. Mudie for 'Snake' by Ian Mudie; Mrs A. M. Walsh for 'The New Boy' by John Walsh; Mrs Hodgson and Macmillan, London and Basingstoke, for 'Stupidity Street' by Ralph Hodgson from *Collected Poems* by Ralph Hodgson; A. P. Watt Ltd for 'Celery', 'Further Reflection on Parsley', 'Birthday on the Beach', 'First Limick', 'What's the Use?', 'The Canary', 'Please Pass the Biscuit', 'The Strange Case of Mr Wood's Frustration or A Team That Won't Be Beaten Better Stay off the Field', 'The Bat', 'The Dog', and 'The Ostrich' by Ogden Nash; Richard Rieu, Executor of the Estate of the Late Dr E. V. Rieu for 'The Flattered Flying Fish' by E. V. Rieu; John Johnson for 'In Memory of Yuri Gargarin' by George Barker; John Heath-Stubbs for the extract from 'Cosmic Poem' published by Turret Book Publishers; David Holbrook for 'The Car under the Steamhammer'.

Index of Poems

Index of Poets

M1049